HOW STUDENTS
UNDERSTAND THE PAST

HOW STUDENTS UNDERSTAND THE PAST

From Theory to Practice

M. ELAINE DAVIS

ALTAMIRA PRESS
A Division of Rowman & Littlefield Publishers, Inc.
Walnut Creek • Lanham • New York • Toronto • Oxford

ALTAMIRA PRESS
A division of Rowman & Littlefield Publishers, Inc.
1630 North Main Street, #367
Walnut Creek, CA 94596
www.altamirapress.com

Rowman & Littlefield Publishers, Inc.
A wholly owned subsidary of The Rowman & Littlefield Publishing Group, Inc.
4501 Forbes Boulevard, Suite 200
Lanham, MD 20706

PO Box 317
Oxford
OX2 9RU, UK

Copyright © 2005 by AltaMira Press

British Library Cataloguing in Publication Information Available

Library of Congress Cataloging-in-Publication Data

Davis, M. Elaine.
    How students understand the past : from theory to practice / M. Elaine Davis.
        p. cm.
    Includes bibliographical references and index.
    ISBN 0-7591-0042-X (alk. paper) — ISBN 0-7591-0043-8 (alk. paper)
    1. History—Study and teaching. I. Title.

    D16.2.D35 2005
    907'.1—dc22

                                                                2004017617

Printed in the United States of America

♾™ The paper used in this publication meets the minimum requirements of American National Standard for Information Sciences—Permanence of Paper for Printed Library Materials, ANSI/NISO Z39.48-1992.

CONTENTS

Tables and Figures

Acknowledgments

IT SEEMS THAT THIS BOOK BEGAN a very long time ago because it grew from my doctoral dissertation, which I completed at the University of North Carolina–Chapel Hill in 1997. Fortunately, I have had the opportunity to think and learn much more about the topic since then, so the final version is quite different from the original.

There are a number of people who provided support along this path from dissertation to book whom I wish to thank. Dr. George Noblit, who was my graduate advisor at Carolina, deserves a great deal of credit for creating the kind of academic climate that nurtures student voice and stimulates independent thought. His approach to educational research and advocacy for qualitative methods has given me tools for examining questions that matter. The other members of my graduate committee, Drs. Glenn Hinson, Dwight Rogers, Vin Steponaitis, and Alan Tom, enriched this work with their thoughtful comments and diverse perspectives. Two of these members deserve a special note of thanks. Glenn Hinson taught me that ethnography truly is an art and that it should always be grounded in respect for the communities and individuals with whom we work. This strongly influenced how I viewed the role of the students in the case study described in part II and is ever present in my work at the Crow Canyon Archaeological Center. I am grateful to Dwight Rogers for his friendly encouragement over the years and his always fine example of caring in education.

There are numerous ways in which the Crow Canyon Archaeological Center has contributed to this work, starting with showing me many years ago that a passion for education and archaeology could coexist and that I could form a career around them. During the dissertation research, the center provided partial funding and assisted me in identifying schools with which I could conduct the study.

In the years since, as director of education at Crow Canyon, I have received enthusiastic support for turning the dissertation into this book. Dr. Ricky Lightfoot, the Center's president and CEO, has provided constant encouragement through the years and it is highly likely that this book would not have happened without his belief in, and commitment to, archaeology education. My friend and colleague, Margie Connolly, has filled in for me on many occasions so that I could finish whatever phase of this project that I was currently working on. I am also indebted to the education staff at Crow Canyon who have, over the years, helped me think about the important questions in teaching the past. They work many long hours in their commitment to enlarging the public's understanding of history in the Southwest.

Finally, I wish to thank friends and family members for support that came in many shapes and sizes but always at the right time. I am grateful beyond words to my mother, Thelma Rich Franklin, for her support of all my educational pursuits and for instilling in me a love of learning. Richard Davis has, over the years, listened to my many concerns related to this project; I am thankful for his patience and encouragement.

My great friend and mentor, Dr. Patricia Shane, has helped me in so many ways, from showing up at my door with care packages during the tedious days of the dissertation, to providing me with employment while in graduate school. I also owe many thanks to Dr. Terry Roberts who read the manuscript for this book and provided thoughtful and constructive commentary, and continued to be my friend even when I didn't always follow his advice.

Introduction

History: A Narrative of Past Events[1]

HISTORY IS MADE. It is made by historians, by archaeologists, by museums, by filmmakers and writers, by senior citizens, and by small children. The past is constructed over and over again by every being who has the ability to think back or to imagine a time before now. The formalizing of history through oral tradition or written documentation has taken place for thousands of years, probably for as long as language has provided humans with a mechanism for referring back. History appears to be as intellectually fundamental to humans as counting and curiosity. The past matters to us.

History is commonly associated with the written past; throughout this book I use the term to refer to the entire human past. The more narrow definition carries a hidden message; it implies that an unwritten past is not legitimate and that the written stories of the past are complete, accurate, and objective. Such an understanding of history denies the past of many groups of people; over time, it can work to erase their past.

Given that history is a narrative of past events and that multiple narratives exist, controversy and disagreement abound. This is particularly true when history is forced to compete for taxpayers' dollars or a portion of the school day. The problem is multifaceted. Traditionally, history education in the United States has had fairly narrow boundaries and the methods for presenting and teaching it have often been as controversial as the content itself. Whether history should be a set of names, dates, and events, or an intellectual inquiry into the past has been debated since public schooling in the United States began.

Compounding the problem of how history is portrayed and taught in the United States is the general erasure of history's authors from the stories that are constructed. This has often applied to the way that the past has been displayed in museums as well as to the stories of the past that have appeared in textbooks. When those who construct the past are hidden from view, history takes on a faceless authority and is elevated to the level of unquestionable truth.

Finally, history education is difficult because so little is understood about how knowledge of the past is constructed. In recent years, the situation has improved and there is a growing interest in how students, teachers, and other members of the public perceive and use the past. Scholars such as Sam Wineburg, Linda Levstik, and Keith Barton have conducted some particularly important work in historical cognition. Such studies are critical to advancing our understanding of how perceptions of the past are formed and discovering how different kinds of experiences affect conceptual development.

How Students Understand the Past deals directly with the construction of historical knowledge by examining ways that people can, and do, make meaning of the past. In this book, I discuss the importance of contemporary learning theory and educational research to the development of effective programs in both formal and informal history education programs. History education research in the United States has frequently focused on what Americans don't know about history. I argue that such projects have been formed around the wrong question; we should be asking what people *do* know about the past. Neither children nor adults are empty vessels where ideas about the human past are concerned. This is not to say that the views of the past are always accurate or that public interests are more important than those held by professionals. I am simply saying that what teachers, exhibit designers, and other educators think they are teaching about the past is not necessarily what is learned. Investigations that reveal the kinds of information about the past that people remember, that show how concepts about the past are formed, and that demonstrate how the past speaks to the present can provide a much needed research base for informing history education in both formal and informal settings. To that end, *How Students Understand the Past* introduces the idea of the learner as an agent in constructing the past and it demonstrates how educational research is essential for gaining an understanding of privately held views of the past.

How Students Understand the Past is written for anyone whose responsibility it is to teach about the human past; this includes schoolteachers, museum educators, archaeologists, and historians. It is organized into three sections. Each section has a different focus and even though they are interrelated, each might also stand alone as a discreet piece. As such, the order in which the book is read is left up to the reader. Part I is about the teaching and learning of history and includes the theoretical background for examining the case study in part II. Readers who are only interested in the case study in part II, rather than the book in its entirety will, I argue, still need information from the first section to fully understand my interpretation of the case study. However, they might choose to use part I as a resource rather than read the full section. Part III might be seen as the applied section of the book in that it takes the points brought forth in the case study and provides three program examples of these principles in practice. For the reader who is only interested in practice and is unconcerned with the foundation that provides the rationale for practice, part III might prove useful as a stand-alone piece.

Part I consists of two chapters. In chapter 1, I discuss the importance of history and its various uses. I also provide the reader with my own history as it relates to this work and to history and archaeology education in general. Honesty in scholarship begins, I believe, with context. Thus, I offer my own history as a vital aspect of the context for the ideas, beliefs, theories, questions, and assertions that appear on the pages of this book. Chapter 2 considers some of the theoretical issues relevant to learning history, such as cognitive development, the construction of knowledge, and the act of interpretation.

The chapters in part II are a detailed account of a research project I conducted to investigate the ways in which fourth-grade students in the American Southwest were constructing their knowledge of Pueblo history. Pseudonyms are used for all participants, as well as for their towns and institutions, with the exception of the Crow Canyon Archaeological Center, located in Cortez, Colorado.

In part III, I draw from my own research, as well as the literature, to give examples of the kinds of educational practice that are designed to engage learners in the study of human history. The last chapter provides practical information regarding assessment and research in historical understanding.

The research project I discuss in part II was conducted in 1996 for my doctoral dissertation. At that time, I was a graduate student in the School of Education at the University of North Carolina in Chapel Hill. I assumed the position of director of education at Crow Canyon in 1997 after my research was completed. At the time of the research project, my position with the center was that of research associate. Prior to that, I was involved with Crow Canyon as an intern in their education department, as a fellowship recipient, and as a participant in their public archaeology programs.

My discussion of historical thinking is situated within the world of archaeology education for several reasons. First of all, I am personally fascinated with archaeological research. I have worked on archaeological projects in the southeastern and the southwestern United States. I am drawn to the discipline because I see it as being critical to expanding our knowledge of the human past. This certainly applies to the majority of human history for which no written records exist, but also for the more recent past for which written records are available. I say this because, unfortunately, oppression is a part of the fabric of human history and those who were the subjects of oppression have generally not had the opportunity to participate in the authorship of the history books nor have they, until the last couple of decades, been systematically involved in the interpretation of the past in museums or other informal settings. Thus, archaeological research can serve to enlighten and present a fuller understanding of the past even when historical records are available. I am also drawn to archaeology because artifacts and archaeological sites are direct physical links to those who created them. The past is abstract and can be extremely difficult to pull into one's own sphere of experience. The physical objects on which archaeological research depends help make the past real and they can create a very tangible bridge to the present.

Some of the same issues that cause unrest in the discipline of history cause problems in archaeological research. Many of the difficulties center around the question of who owns the past; with archaeology, this includes the actual physical remains of the past. There is also disagreement over who has the authority to construct narratives about the past and whose narratives are legitimate. These issues, along with a history of objectification of Native peoples by anthropologists— particularly in the early decades of the twentieth century—have led to tensions between Native Americans and archaeologists. I hope that these challenges can be successfully resolved and I believe that the benefits of doing so far outweigh the costs. Archaeological research and oral tradition are both essential for placing the past of Native Americans and other disenfranchised people within the frame of legitimized history. This is a goal worth working for.

Another reason I have chosen to focus my research on archaeology education rather than on the more traditional world of history education is because archaeology education is a relatively young discipline. Being only a couple of decades old, archaeology education has not yet established a canon that defines accepted content and practices. This means that it is still a very malleable field; it also means that there is, unfortunately, not a lot of understanding about what constitutes best practice. To a degree, archaeological knowledge has been shared with the American public for at least a century. However, this was generally not with the larger public but, rather, the elite, the well educated, and, in a few instances, a more general audience who happened to live in close proximity to dramatic sites or large museums. In many cases, these earlier endeavors were not so much about educating the public as they were about awing them (Bennett 1995). The discipline of archeology itself was still in an immature state in the early 1900s and some would argue that both the research efforts and public involvement did more harm than good.

One of the most significant changes in sharing the past with the public in the United States was initiated by the Society for American Archaeology (SAA) in the mid-1980s when the organization identified public education as a primary concern. The establishment of a Public Education Committee (PEC) within the organization followed this recognition. As a result, numerous workshops have been conducted for various segments of the public, a network of public archaeology coordinators has been established, and an array of print material has been produced. The society and its members have accomplished a great deal over a short period of time. A highly positive aspect of many public archaeology programs is that they contain some kind of explanation regarding the research methods that archaeologists use. In other words, many archaeologists have recognized that, along with teaching about their discoveries, they also need to help members of the general public understand the research process.

One of the difficulties with archaeology education has to do with who is doing it and how well prepared they might be to meet the needs of a nonprofessional audience. Most archaeologists don't have an academic background in the field of education, thus, their knowledge in areas such as human cognition and instructional methods may be somewhat lacking. To address this problem, many archaeologists who serve on the SAA/PEC have formed partnerships with teachers and other professional educators in their communities. The world of American archaeology education is, however, much larger than the SAA/PEC. Many of the archaeology education programs and curricula that have been produced in the United States are uninformed by contemporary learning theory or effective instructional methodologies. In other cases, the curricula are designed by educators who are masters of pedagogy but have a poor understanding of the discipline of archaeology.

As is often true in other disciplines, it has sometimes been assumed that knowledge of the subject matter is all that is needed for effective instruction. This assumption almost inevitably leads to the development of deadly dull curricula in which the only reason students become engaged is because of some extrinsic reward, such as getting good grades or building a strong résumé for college. A sounder approach to teaching about the human past would be to develop curricula that are informed by a well-developed research base. This book will have achieved something important if it inspires those involved in history and archaeology education to systematically examine teaching and learning in these fields and to make a commitment to contribute to a solid body of research upon which educational practice can rely.

Note

1. *Webster's II: New Riverside University Dictionary* (The Riverside Publishing Company, 1994), 584.

TEACHING AND LEARNING HISTORY I

History Matters   I

The past is myself, my own history, the seed of my present thoughts, the mold of my present disposition.[1]

—R. L. STEVENSON (QUOTED IN E. TONKIN 1992)

Some of these children feel like they are less than nobody.[2]
(Comment on why young black Americans need African American history.)

—ELLA A. WILLIAMS-VINSON (1995)

Introduction

THE PRESENT IS FOREVER DISAPPEARING, just as we focus on it, it moves away. The future is no more than a probability, a less-than-certain promise of tomorrow. And so we are left with only the past from which to make sense of our world. What happens when we have no history, when we cannot find a way to enter into the narratives of the past? What present disposition will be fashioned from the empty past of those less-than-nobody children that Williams-Vinson speaks of? This book considers the interconnectedness of history with culture and with self. It takes a particularly close look at how concepts of the past are constructed and how they are influenced by educational experiences and by instruction.

That history does indeed matter is an underlying foundation of this work. That all language systems hold within them a structure for allowing the speaker to refer back (Tonkin 1992) leads to a further assumption—history matters to all peoples and it has always mattered. A study with 1,500 American adults, conducted by historians Roy Rosenzweig and David Thelen, indicates that the past is a very real part of most people's lives and that it provides a foundation for understanding the present as well as for anticipating the future (1998). The Society for American Archaeology (SAA) sponsored a Harris Poll that was conducted with another group of 1,500 Americans to determine what general concepts they had regarding archaeology and the human past, particularly the deep past, which is often referred to by archaeologists and historians as prehistory. Based on the results, researchers in this study concluded that the majority of Americans are interested in learning about the past, they believe that archaeology is important, and they place great value on the parts of the past that are revealed through archaeology. In addition, the research project also shows that Americans believe archaeology should be included in precollege curricula (Ramos and Duganne 2000).

Interest in the past is not an American phenomenon. A British study, also involving 1,500 adults, showed that 79 percent of the respondents thought that the past was definitely worth knowing about and another 12 percent thought it probably worth knowing about (Merriman 1991). The popularity of film documentaries on topics as varied as the American Civil War and the history of baseball provide further evidence that large numbers of people consider the human past to be important.

It is more difficult to find evidence that history matters in American schools or, more specifically, that it matters to the students in those schools: "High School students hate history. When they list their favorite subjects, history invariably comes in last. Students consider history the most irrelevant of twenty-one subjects taught in high school" (Loewen 1995:1).

In the same vein, Mihaly Csikszentmihalyi notes that, "Typically, students rate history the worst subject for engagement" (Scherer 2003:4). Will Fitzhugh identifies a lack of understanding regarding the nature of history and the absence of real historical research from the educational program as being central to the problem (Fitzhugh 2004).

Rosenzweig and Thelen's study uncovered similar attitudes about history as a school subject:

> While respondents spoke of films and books with indifference, they described studying history in vividly negative terms. When we asked some of them to "pick one word or phrase to describe your experiences with history classes in elementary or high school," almost three fifths chose such words as "irrelevant," "incomplete," "dry," or, most commonly, "boring." In the entire study, respondents almost never described encounters with the past as boring—except when they talked about school. [1998:31]

The participants in Rosenzweig and Thelen's study were adults (eighteen years of age and older), so they were reflecting on their own schooling rather than speaking of a present experience. And, considering that this population attended high school more than ten years ago, there is a legitimate argument that they don't reflect the current state of history in the schools. In fact, I hesitate to reference their study for fear that it will alienate history teachers. However, even if we could imagine that formal classroom history has dramatically improved over the last decade, I argue that the attitudes of the respondents in this study are worth paying attention to. The populations that the sample group represents are the voters and policy makers of today. Thus, even if their perceptions of history education are outdated, and this is debatable, they are still in the position of influencing decisions that directly impact history in schools as well as in informal settings.

The perspective of the participants in studies like the ones cited above resonate with me because I was one of those high school students who could not connect with history as it was taught in school. In my teenaged mind, the stories told through the sanctioned history of school textbooks were, to use Loewen's term, lies, and that those who told them were promoting a hidden agenda. I saw school history as ignoring the stories of real people and masking the intent of its authors, which was, from my teenaged perspective, to appropriate the past for the purpose of reinforcing a national narrative. This history seemed a lie to me because it was reductive and simplistic; it was a narrative without the tension of disagreement and difference. It could not be the past of my present experience because I lived in a world of competing agendas, a world in which there was not one ideology but many, and others that were continually emerging. The past of my school history books was a narrative of cardboard characters with painted-on facades; they had no depth and no heart. Such one-dimensional figures could not have accomplished what the stories credited them with. Deceit and control were the forces that I perceived to be at work in the making of our national history. I was a teenager who did not like being manipulated and I resisted—I simply didn't listen. While I admit that my rebellious teenaged perspective was somewhat biased and narrow, I believe it was not atypical for teens at that time; perhaps it would not be atypical today.

Like many other teens, I also found school history to be boring but I was not bored with the past. There were isolated events in my schooling where the past intersected in meaningful ways with my present. In the sixth grade, my teacher, Mr. Upchurch, read Homer's *Odyssey* to our class. I was mesmerized by the stories. I could see Penelope unraveling the tapestry each night and could imagine the sweet agony of Odysseus, tied to the mast of his ship, listening to the song of the Sirens.

In the 1960s, I experienced the deaths of contemporary heroes. The assassination of John F. Kennedy caused me to see leaders as real people with real families. I was in Mrs. Green's fourth-grade classroom when our school principal announced that the president had been shot in Dallas, Texas, and that he was dead. I was a child in 1963 and my heart went out to Caroline Kennedy and her little brother, John, as they bravely stood beside their father's—the president's—flag-draped coffin. They were close to my age and I imagined that I understood how they felt. I remember not having school again until days later, after President Kennedy was buried. I do not remember celebrating my freedom from the classroom but I do remember mourning and seeing the rest of the nation mourn. I knew I was witnessing history and reflection on that experience tells me that a fact on a time line cannot adequately convey the grand drama of a nation in pain.

When I was in the eighth grade, the assassinations of Dr. Martin Luther King Jr. and Robert Kennedy opened my eyes to a history of discrimination and social injustice in America. The newspaper and television coverage of these assassinations caused me to think about the history of oppression in the United States and to see how the threads of past wrongs are so painfully present in the tapestry of modern times.

In saying that history matters, I am saying that we cannot understand the present state of our world without looking to the world of yesterday and the day before. Without the explanatory power of preceding events, the world of today can seem highly irrational. In saying history matters, I am also saying that we value the past and we value the lives of those who came before us. The stories of the past that captured my attention as a youth were not stories of glory and splendor but those that connected in some way with the common realities of the present. In viewing the past through the lens of the present, I was able to establish meaningful connections; I could find a history that mattered.

History and Power

If you are convinced you have never done anything, you can never do anything.[3]

—MALCOLM X (1965)

The setting is a fifth-grade classroom. A twelve-foot time line is on display, with each foot representing one thousand years of human occupation in the Americas. Students are generating a list of historical events from memory and locating them on the time line. After a dozen or so have been placed, a clear pattern has emerged. Other than one lone point representing the crossing of the Bering Land Bridge about 12,000 years ago, the events all rest on the last six inches of the time line— the time since Columbus. Students explain this pattern either by saying that there was no change in those other years, that we do not know anything about those years, or that nothing happened. They know something is wrong. Their own ability to reason and think logically tells them this is not so.

Over the last fifty years, the excluded pasts of African Americans, Native Americans, women, and others have been brought more fully into public consciousness. Changes in relation to diversity have also appeared in school textbooks, but it is important to ask, "To what degree?"

A study of history textbooks from the 1960s, 1980s, and 1990s confirms that women have gained ground in American history texts over the last forty years but that, "Writers of history texts have not configured their view of history to show that women in the U. S., as the Chinese proverb has it, have held up at least one half the sky" (Clark, Allard, and Mahoney 2004:57–62). In fact, the authors of the study state that the history books don't even come close. They found that the ratio of women to men listed in the indexes of these books had climbed from about 5 percent in the 1960s to only 16 percent by the late 1990s. While this is certainly progress, it is far from "half the sky." Would the same group of fifth graders who constructed the time line assume this means that we do not know what women did, or, perhaps, that they did nothing?

History, limited to its disciplinary definition, privileges the past that is represented by written text. This sort of document-based history carries an authoritative voice; the storyteller who took pen to page and made history often becomes invisible. When we lose the connection between a story and its origin, it enters the realm of mythology. Roland Barthes (1972) speaks of mythology as depoliticized speech—symbols severed from their history and divorced from their origin. When this happens, we tend to mistake the way we perceive things with the way things are. The stories of our American past may be considered depoliticized in the sense that the storytellers are often hidden. This has often been as true for museum exhibits and other kinds of informal education as it has been for history textbooks. The myth is woven through an authoritative voice that conceals the assumptions the stories are grounded in and we are presented with a past that is taken as fact. The myth precludes a more critical history. When we fail to recognize that many historical characters rose to power within systems that privileged some and oppressed far more, we develop a skewed understanding of the past. Unfortunately, the exclusion of certain groups of people, and the unwritten past in general, appears to be a common practice around the globe: "There are examples of school textbooks from all parts of the world that ignore contemporary understanding of the prehistoric past" (MacKenzie and Stone 1990:3).

Unfortunately, while much has been learned about the indigenous past of Uruguay in the last three decades, this knowledge continues to be excluded from the official primary school textbooks. Consequently, the indigenous past and its role in the formation of the national community remain largely absent and unexplored. [Mañosa 1999:7]

Some have suggested that history, as taught in the nation's schools and other institutions, is little more than a hegemonic narrative that works to reproduce privilege. Or, to paraphrase the words of Malcolm X (Loewen 1995), to convince certain groups of people that they have never accomplished anything of importance and are, thus, incapable of anything noteworthy in the future. And, conversely, it works to send the message to certain other groups that they are the inheritors and progenitors of a legacy of greatness. Joyce Appleby, Lynn Hunt, and Margaret Jacob state that, "From the revolution to the early part of the twentieth century, this (American) history came from a small, well-established sub-set of the nation's population, and it invariably flattered the members of the elite" (1994). Assuming that such an appropriation of the past exists, how effective it is has been in terms of social and cultural reproduction is a matter for debate. If James W. Loewen and others are correct in saying that students find little meaning in their school history courses and that they remember precious little (Loewen 1995:1), how would the historical myths be working to maintain the status quo? Perhaps the answer rests not so much in the history that is presented but, rather, in the history that is omitted. Might this help explain the student responses on the time line previously described?

Making History

We see things not as they are but as we are.

—ANAIS NIN (QUOTED IN LOEWEN 1995:232)

The problem of improving history education is complex; it includes problems with curricular content as well as instructional methodology. The National Standards for History call for a more critical approach to history instruction, placing increased emphasis on the use of original documents and multiple sources of information (National Center for History in the Schools 1996). This appears to be a step toward reform but may actually be little more than a face-lift. It gives the appearance of doing something different and it does, within a very narrow definition of the human past. It is a broader look at the past of those who have written their stories, but it still excludes the past of many Americans who were denied access to formal education and to literacy until the earlier part of the twentieth century. Education became institutionalized in the United States in the late 1800s and, while it has often been referred to as the great equalizer, it has not been and still is not an equitable system. The inclusion of original documents and multiple sources does broaden our perspective of human history, but only to the extent that the constraints of a written past will allow. There is no real reform in such actions because they serve to maintain an inequitable system rather than transform it.

The adherence to a document-based past prohibits change in pedagogy as well as in the content of the history curriculum. Over the last twenty years, both oral history and archaeology have found their way into public history education but neither has managed to play a significant role. Most programs have been the result of grass-roots efforts initiated by creative educators, archaeologists, and historians, or by professional organizations working outside the mainstream of education. An important example is the Foxfire project, which began in the 1970s with the efforts of one gifted teacher in Rabun County, Georgia. Foxfire is a program for involving high school students in collecting and publishing the oral histories from their communities. Foxfire has endured in northern Georgia despite an unfortunate scandal involving the teacher who founded it. Students who have participated in these classes have found not only a love of doing history but also a sense of pride in their own heritage.

Even though Foxfire has been replicated in independent classrooms nationwide, oral history has not been well integrated into formal history education in the United States. Traditional historians have often been critical of oral history, saying that it only has the power to reach back a few generations. This argument might hold true within communities where the oral tradition is not valued—when stories are not told we may lose the skills for telling them. However, where oral tradition and storytelling are respected and where they occupy a critical role in the transmission of knowledge, narratives can be maintained across many generations. Often, objects that have become the treasured artifacts of a family or of a culture function as historical texts that help carry the narratives through time in a tangible way. In some cultures, places on the landscape serve the same function.

Archaeologists, like historians, seek to illuminate the human past. They attempt to identify patterns and departures from those patterns in the behavior of humans across time and space. However, rather than the written word or oral tradition, archaeologists look to a culture's material remains for information regarding their lifestyles, their actions, and their interactions with others. Archaeological research fits most closely within a scientific paradigm. The stories rendered are admittedly partial, they are jigsaw puzzles with missing pieces and sometimes these pieces are revealed as incorrect in the light of further investigation. A culture's past is in no way fully represented on an archaeological site. The survival of material culture is subject to climatic conditions and to disturbance by humans and other animals. The record that archaeologists are able to examine is often only a reflection of those things that a group of people chose not to take with them when they moved to a new home.

Archaeologists often focus their research on the histories of those who have been marginalized and excluded from more traditional approaches to understanding the past. These histories are layered in the soil beneath our feet and there exists but one text for each story. Once read, it is destroyed. Each reading thereafter is but a reconstruction, subject to the accuracy and care given to the recording of the original version. Because archaeological excavation is a destructive process, one might view an archaeological site as a book in which each page disintegrates just as it is revealed. While everyone can probably recall stories of Howard Carter and his glorious discoveries in Egypt, the real treasures an archaeologist finds are not the "wonderful things" of which Carter spoke; they are the stories that are told through these wonderful things.

Archaeology has remained largely outside the general course of study in American schools. Where it has entered in, it has been in the form of content—the products of archaeological research—such as life in ancient Egypt, but not the processes archaeologists use for knowing about the past. In recent years, there has been a movement to teach both archaeological process and content to the general public, particularly precollege audiences. This initiative comes from professional archaeologists who have recognized a need to relate their work to the larger public. These efforts grew, at least initially, from the realization that cultural resources were being destroyed at an alarming rate and that a caring public would be the only way to save the past for the future.

One outcome of this concern for educating the public about archaeology is an increase in the quantity of archaeology education materials and programs that are available. In many cases, working with the public has become a general requirement of professional archaeologists. Educational opportunities available to the public are fairly diverse, from site tours and lectures, to actually involving members of the public in archaeological research. Regardless of the nature of the activity, there is generally high praise for outreach programs. These initiatives seem to be working in terms of public satisfaction. In other words, there is ample evidence that those who participate in the programs enjoy them. This is important but it seems that, from an educational perspective, more information is needed. What does it mean when an educational program is said to be working? Learning should be fun, but having an enjoyable experience does not necessarily equate to learning. This is particularly true for those situations where participation is completely voluntary. For example, members of archaeological and historical societies often attend programs that provide general information about topics in which they are already well versed. The same could be said of children who tend to gravitate toward topics that are at once exotic and familiar; mummies and ancient Egypt are good examples. Children will often consume everything in their path that is related to these topics but they are far less likely to venture into new territory or to seek out information that contradicts their privately held concepts. Education should guide learners into new territory, it should cause them to examine their knowledge, as well as their conceptual understandings, and present them with new information.

There are a number of reasons for not examining what the public learns through archaeology education programs. Assessment requires funding; archaeologists often struggle just to pay for the basic requirements of conducting research, such as analysis and curation. The lack of assessment within archaeology education is also due to the fact that, in many situations, archaeologists work with the public because they are required to do so but there are often no expectations regarding actual learning outcomes. Many of the early archaeology education programs only had one serious objective, which was to build stewardship and increase preservation of archaeological sites. Because it is so difficult to evaluate the effectiveness of any type of ethics education, assessment of these programs has been problematic.

Finally, some archaeologists have just not cared whether the general public learned anything beyond keeping their hands off archaeological sites. These archaeologists are involved in public education because they are required to do so or because they have learned how to pay for archaeological research by claiming to have an educational agenda. Funding archaeological research through the involvement of the public is not only appropriate it is innovative and can have many positive outcomes. However, when archaeological research is paired with public education, it is essential that the educational mission be highly valued; this is important to the quality of the educational endeavor and to the integrity of the field of archaeology.

The history of anthropology is riddled with the objectification of others for the advancement of the profession and individuals within it. Fortunately, the profession has turned a critical eye on itself in recent decades and it is no longer considered ethical to conduct anthropological research in such a self-interested fashion. To misappropriate public education for the purpose of funding archaeological research, with no sincere commitment to actually educate the public, is wrong and it puts archaeology education at risk. Such efforts generally result in weak curricula and ineffective programs that are viewed badly by professional educators.

Understanding how the past is constructed in the minds of individuals and how constructions are influenced by variables such as age, culture, ethnicity, and instruction is essential to the improvement of history and archaeology education. It seems unlikely that everyone understands information about the past in the same way or will find the same meaning in it. The interpretation of history in terms of self and identity is a consistent theme in the quotations that introduce some of the sections in this chapter. But do we appropriate the past in order to construct self, or do we appropriate aspects of our identity in an attempt to place ourselves in the continuum of human experience—are we just trying to belong? These are not simple questions, and it is not likely that they will be answered once and for all. However, if education about the human past is to advance, we must have a pedagogy that is grounded in a stronger theoretical understanding than, "it works." To approach such an understanding, it is essential that the questions posed here be explored in the context of real learning events and through the perspectives of the learners in those events.

My History Matters

On a hot August day in 1982, I ran out of gas in Bluff, Utah, a small town whose economy is supported by tourists on their way to canyon country and by river runners who navigate the San Juan. I was on a road trip. My husband and brother were traveling with me; we were in the tenth day of a two-week swing through the great American West. We were headed to the Grand Canyon when we ran out of gas. There were two gas stations in Bluff, but neither could provide assistance; the electricity was out all over town, meaning that no gas could be pumped. We spent the night in Bluff, captive tourists, as it were.

For reasons I still don't understand, the sixteen hours spent in Bluff took on a very surreal quality. A series of odd events piggybacked on one another, forming a composite that I can only describe as ominous. I had a sense that we had walked, or perhaps coasted, into someone else's story. We had entered a narrative that was already in progress and could not find a logical context for the events we witnessed. During our hiatus in Bluff, we ate dinner in a gas station, saw our first Native American petroglyphs, were confronted by a strange and angry man on a lonely desert road, and witnessed the grief of our innkeeper as she received word of her son's death. It is difficult to relate how these events affected my perception of that time spent in Bluff, but cumulatively they contributed to an unshakable sense that an ill wind was blowing through that tiny corner of southeast Utah.

There is a hesitation to tell stories such as this, first because you really had to be there—the atmosphere cannot adequately be conveyed in the retelling. Second, there is a risk of losing credibility; it is a story that just sounds flaky. Regardless, the events of that experience served to carve Bluff, Utah, into my memory.

Six years later, in June 1988, I was in a bookstore shopping for a Father's Day present. At that time, I was an elementary schoolteacher in Chapel Hill, North Carolina. In my search for a gift, I picked up a novel written by one of my father's favorite writers and began thumbing through the pages. Just after the title page was a map—of Bluff, Utah, and the surrounding area. My night in Bluff came flooding back and I found myself purchasing the novel. It was a mystery that centered around the prehistory of the Southwest, and an archaeologist was the main character. The plot was actually quite farfetched but I found myself drawn into the underlying story, the story of a people who had lived in the Northern San Juan region for centuries but by A.D. 1300 had completely vacated the area. I finished the novel but I wanted to know more about this cultural group that most people refer to as Anasazi. I located an old issue of *National Geographic* that was devoted to studies of these ancient Pueblo people. The articles led me to other books and resources, which, in turn, led me to the Southwest to visit sites where some of their villages had been located. Each opportunity for learning left me with new questions and each one laid the foundation for the next. I became hooked on learning about the human past through archaeology and the rest, as they say, is history. It is my history and, because this book is about the teaching and learning of history, my history matters.

I can make no interpretative leaps regarding the significance of my night in Bluff. I can only observe that, had it never occurred, if the gas pumps had been working, if we had gassed up in Blanding or chosen a different route, if the stay in Bluff had just seemed like another night in a small tourist town, my life at this point would be dramatically different. The map in the novel could not have sparked my interest; I would have selected a different book for my father; or I might have moved on to another store and bought a tie. History does matter and an individual's past, as well as a community's past, helps carve the course to their present. What we have been provides insight into who we are and how we view events in our world. My experiences with history as a youth, my self-label as a progressive educator, and my passion for archaeology are powerful lenses that I must continually be conscious of and that the reader of this book should be conscious of. The instant I fail to recognize these influences on my work is the point at which they cease to be lenses and function instead as blinders.

Notes

1. Quoted by Christabel Bielenberg 1989 in her autobiography, *The Past Is Myself*. Referenced by Elizabeth Tonkin, *Narrating Our Pasts* (Cambridge: Cambridge University Press, 1992):1.

2. Ella A. Williams-Vinson 1995. Audio-taped interview for the *Southern Oral History Collection*, UNC-Chapel Hill.

3. Malcolm X, from Gil Noble's film, *Malcolm X* (Carlsbad, CA: CRM Films, 1965). Quoted in James W. Loewen, *Lies My Teacher Told Me* (New York: The New Press, 1995):208.

Thinking Our Way into the Past

2

Introduction

TO APPROACH AN UNDERSTANDING of how learners construct the past, it is important to first discover what they actually know of the past and how they have come to know what they know. Preconceptions regarding past peoples and events are almost always in place before any instruction begins. The preconceptions may or may not concur with scholarly versions of the past and they can be infused with stereotypical images. In trying to ascertain how *young* learners construct the past, it is also important to consider cognitive development and how various theories of development have influenced the teaching of history.

Finally, it must be understood that history is always constructed imperfectly; we can never know the past with complete certainty. The human past is removed in time and, like the human present, is social in nature. Thus, knowledge of the past is always an interpretation of available evidence. In precollege history classes, interpretations of the past are generally conveyed to students through textbooks. However, this doesn't mean that the history learned matches the goals and objectives identified by the authors of those heavy volumes. How students assimilate what they know of the past and how they make meaning of it is their own personal act of interpretation.

To summarize, the question of how learners construct the past implicates three strands of inquiry that deal respectively with social, cognitive, and cultural issues. This chapter addresses these strands by discussing constructivist learning theory, cognitive development, and the complex act of interpretation. Readers from different professional orientations will have varying degrees of familiarity with these topics. Teachers, for example, probably have a more well-developed understanding of constructivism than archaeologists have, and archaeologists are likely to have a deeper understanding of interpretation than most teachers have. Because *How Students Understand the Past* is written for a broad audience, encompassing teachers and archaeologists, as well as history and museum educators, it is necessary to include this discussion about cognition and knowledge construction. It is admittedly brief but I hope it will suffice as an introduction of key concepts and terms that form the theoretical foundation for the case study in part II.

Constructivism

The literature on constructivism is immense and varied for constructivism is not one theory but a set of related theories that attempt to explain the nature of knowledge. The common thread that ties these theories together is the belief that people create knowledge and that knowledge is influenced by values and culture. This perspective may be contrasted with the behaviorist view of learning that, for many decades, formed the foundation of traditional approaches to schooling in the United States. Behaviorists view knowledge as being outside the learner and consider the purpose of education to be the instilling of an accepted body of information that has been previously established by experts (Scheurman 1998).

Although there are numerous variations on constructivist theory, there are two fundamental positions: social and cognitive. Jean Piaget has been a powerful voice in the area of cognitive constructivism. Piaget is best known for his belief in universal structures of knowledge and developmental stages of human cognition. Key to Piaget's theory of learning is the notion that knowledge is acquired as a result of the individual's attempt to maintain intellectual equilibrium. This process begins when an individual encounters some obstacle to the assimilation or accommodation of new information, which Piaget identified as perturbations. These perturbations, also referred to as conflicts or contradictions, prevent the person from reaching a goal or from using or incorporating new elements into a scheme; the result is cognitive disequilibrium. Regulations intended to compensate the perturbations are produced; these, in turn, generate new constructions and move the individual back to a state of cognitive equilibrium.

To illustrate, a fourth-grade student from Texas who was visiting Crow Canyon Archaeological Center was having trouble untangling his generic—one might say stereotypical—understanding of "Indian." As with many young people, images of Plains Indian dress and lifestyle were dominating his concept of who Native Americans are, and were. He was at the Center for a week-long program with his school group. On the fourth day of his stay, the youngster and his class were touring an excavated, and somewhat rebuilt, twelfth-century Pueblo village. On seeing the standing walls of a room block and the associated kiva, the boy excitedly ran up to his Crow Canyon instructor and declared, "This is not a teepee!"

It was an astounding experience for the instructor because she had, from the first lesson with this group, been working to introduce students to Pueblo history and culture. They had seen maps of ancient villages, touched models of ancient houses, and viewed photographs of modern Pueblos. They had participated in a simulated excavation of ancient Pueblo houses and had toured an active archaeological excavation project. Yet, on this, the fourth day of his five-day trip, the student was suddenly amazed to recognize that Indian houses could be something other than a teepee. He knew that he had had a breakthrough in his understanding. In Piagetian terms, he moved through the perturbation and reached cognitive equilibrium. More simply stated, the contradictory information was eventually so overwhelming that he could no longer hold on to his belief that all Indians live in teepees.

Russian psychologist Lev Vygotsky is closely associated with the social constructivist perspective. Vygotsky accepted Piaget's views of how individuals build private understandings through problem solving in a social setting, but he moved beyond the level of the individual to say that knowledge is co-constructed in social contexts, resulting in public understandings of objects and events. From this perspective, knowledge is not objective but is a product of the interactions and agreements of a society. Humor works as an excellent example of this. That which is, or is not, humorous is culturally and, in most cases, temporally situated. Humor generally involves a great deal of insider knowledge and if this is absent, we simply do not "get it." Granted, not all people within a cultural group will agree on what is funny but they will generally understand why certain things are supposed to be funny. Something as simple as the knock-knock joke might meet blank stares in an equatorial village where there may be few walls on dwellings and even fewer doors. From the view of social constructivism, "funny" isn't a given; it is co-constructed out of a particular social/cultural context.

In terms of the history of constructivism, Peter Berger and Thomas Luckman's *The Social Construction of Reality* (1967) stands out as a seminal work. According to Berger and Luckman, the fundamental underlying notion of constructivism is that we carry our past with us and that we are generally not conscious of how our past affects our present concept of reality. Because each individual past is different, it follows that we do not, and cannot, share a common view of reality. Thus, multiple realities exist and knowledge is socially constructed from the perspectives of these disparate realities. Additionally, Berger and Luckman point out that these multiple realities tend to go unrecognized and unacknowledged. From their perspective, everyday life is taken for granted and reality appears already objectified. This position seems somewhat comparable to Pierre Bourdieu's concept of habitus or Barthes's notion of mythologies. Bourdieu defines habitus as "the durably installed generative principles" that produce and reproduce the practices of a class

(Bourdieu 1977). These principles or values are taken for granted and, because they are so embedded, individuals do not question them. Similarly, Barthes (1972) says that when we lose sight of the origins of our beliefs and practices, they take on the characteristics of mythology. When we do not question the way things are, or consciously consider the nature of our social world, we assume that others see the same reality—a reality that appears to be *the* reality.

Research conducted by educational psychologist Sam Wineburg suggests that, whether referring to children or adults, the odds of achieving mature historical understanding are stacked against us. In interviews conducted with high school students and adults, Wineburg found that their natural inclination was to explain historical events in terms of existing beliefs or according to the rules of their culturally bound logic. Even when study participants were presented with evidence that contradicted their existing beliefs, and that they deemed as credible, they continued to stick with their original interpretations. Wineburg sees the problem as being the tension that exists between the familiar and the strange. He says that historical thinking is an unnatural act because of our desire to make the past familiar rather than become amazed by its strangeness (Wineburg 2001). What Wineburg describes seems similar to the problems encountered by other researchers who have looked at how students develop their conceptual understandings in science. Researchers in science education refer to these previously held beliefs as preconceptions or misconceptions and emphasize the necessity of making students aware of their own privately held understandings in order to move them toward conceptual change.

In summary, what I am describing as being a constructivist view would recognize the influence of history, as well as nature, society, and culture on an individual's conceptual development. Instructionally, the constructivist view of learning calls for what C. A. Bowers speaks of as the sociology of knowledge approach. Bowers states that the intent of such a position is to:

> challenge the notion that we can think about curriculum without recognizing that the student's conceptual maps are an important determinant of what is experienced as meaningful. The student's consciousness is not the blank sheet that can be programmed by the way in which the teacher organizes the curriculum. [Bowers 1987:79]

In considering the implications of constructivism for the teaching and learning of history, I will return to the founding proposition that this book rests on—the belief that history is made. A constructivist view of learning not only embraces this notion, it is grounded in it. In thinking of the issues that come to play in constructing the past, I am reminded of the infinite reflections created when we position one mirror before another. The multiple images are connected in an interdependent fashion; when one mirror is removed, the multiple images dissolve.

To apply this metaphor, traditional approaches to teaching the past tend to present historical information as a finished story with one correct version. When many individuals, let's say a classroom, come together, they each bring unique biographies; these individual histories may be seen as the opposing mirror. When these personal histories are brought to bear on narratives of the past, the images created are layered and seemingly endless. To expect twenty-five minds to embrace the original narrative in a comprehensive way is highly unrealistic.

Research into how Americans use the past lends support to a constructivist approach to history education. Americans want to be active participants in the making of history rather than the passive receptacles of a past constructed by others (Rosenzweig and Thelen 1998). The authors of that study envision a participatory historical culture in which authority is shared and where individuals acquire skills to interpret history for themselves. History education that is grounded in this concept of active participation and construction would be what Jerome Bruner refers to as a discipline of understanding the past rather than an account of what happened: "History never simply happens: it is constructed by historians. It is a lame excuse to say that children can't do it" (Bruner 1996:91).

Cognitive Development and the Concept of Time

Time is a highly abstract concept and very few adults, if approached on the street, would be able to supply an adequate definition. Most of us associate time with the concrete objects we use to mark its passing. However, clocks and watches are only mechanical or electronic devices that move or change in a standardized way and at a standardized rate. They are, in fact, fairly recent inventions. Timing devices came into prominence with the industrial revolution and the need to regulate the operation of machines, as well as to structure multiple shifts of workers. Cultures that do not mark the passing of time with some type of mechanical measuring device may relate time to the completion of tasks, to environmental changes, or celestial events. Our difficulty, as educators, in understanding how children conceptualize time is, perhaps, linked to the fact that we know very little about how adults in our society construct time. What we do know is that time is of immense value to the modern world. It is interesting to consider some of the common phrases and expressions that have entered into the English language that include the word time: time is money, killing time, buying time, time waits for no one, use time wisely, no time like the present, time on task, etc. The message is one of efficiency and economy; time in the twenty-first century is a highly valued commodity.

When does the ability to think in more sophisticated ways about time develop? Can children of elementary school age sort out issues of time? Can they link events together across time and recognize causal relationships? Are they capable of historical thinking? These questions have been revisited several times over the past century and it seems that no consensus has been reached. Investigations into how children understand time have been primarily of two varieties—those that grow out of research in the field of cognitive psychology and those that examine the learning of historical information. The influence of Piaget's stage theory of intellectual development on educational design and practice has been of particular importance. Recent efforts to examine the way children understand time and place tend to either dispute a Piagetian framework or adapt aspects of it to conform to more recent studies. A strict interpretation of Piaget's work might not support any study of history in the elementary grades (K–5). The preoperational and concrete-operational stages, as described by Piaget, (associated with five- to nine-year-olds) do not encompass the formation of complex concepts. Thus, in a Piagetian frame, the abstractions essential to historical reasoning would be considered too advanced for the early years of schooling. The scarcity of history education before grade three or four may be a direct reflection of the influence that developmental theory has had on the curriculum.

It does seem, however, that the National History Standards were not developed from a Piagetian frame, as they do include standards for grades K–4. In general, the standards suggest that children should begin learning about family history, only going back a couple of generations, and eventually branch out in their explorations of time and space to include deeper time, other lands, and different cultures (National Center for History in the Schools 1996). Those critical of the application of Piaget's stage theory to the teaching and learning of history have generally centered their critique around three points: (1) that advancement through the stages of cognitive development is highly individual; (2) that advancement can be facilitated through instruction; and (3) that Piaget's theory is appropriate for understanding cognition in the sciences but is not as useful for explaining how children conceptualize social knowledge (Bruner 1996). More recently, research into the ways we understand and conceptualize time has grown out of, but moved beyond, a strictly Piagetian model. Jacques Montangero refers to his diachronic approach as post-Piagetian. He also takes issue with those who would dismiss Piaget as a stage theorist, saying: "This interpretation does not correspond to Piaget's theory whose principal aim was not the description of general stages but the search for organizational forms and functional processes which explain the nature of reasoning and its transformations during development" (Montangero 1996:165).

Montanegro's theoretical position is quite compelling; he defines his approach as constructivist in nature and he uses Piagetian methodology. He distinguishes his work from a Piagetian perspective primarily in that it is absent of any precise description of structure and that the idea of stages is diminished. His work is highly focused on knowledge as it is constructed at the individual level and the aspects of reality that are significant to the individual.

A diachronic approach, according to Montangero, views the present situation as a point or stage in an evolutive process, rather than as an entity that might stand alone in an unchanging state. The assumption here is that the nature of things is to transform. The application of this view to an understanding of cognition involves several steps:

> In the first place, leaving the present through a specific act of decentration which allows subjects to imagine more than they can perceive in the here and now. Second, it involves imagining certain crucial past stages and predicting the possibilities of future change. Third the application of a diachronic approach consists of envisaging the various stages as elements in an evolutive process which displays certain characteristics. Indeed, it is this point that makes the reconstruction or anticipation of past or future stages effective. Fourth, the links established between the stages, thanks to knowledge of the process of transformation, make it possible, in part at least, to explain the present situation in terms of its past stages or future development. [Montangero 1996:165]

Montangero identifies three knowledge types that underlie these four diachronic schemes: axiological, empirical, and organizational; put simply, he is referring to knowledge related to values, the knowledge we construct as a result of our experiences, and the structural knowledge we use to make sense of the information we carry. He asserts that diachronic thinking is a distinct and separate mode of cognition that starts with the appearance of thought and that it is possible to assess this development within an individual. Although his studies only consider diachronic thinking in children between the ages of seven and twelve, he emphasizes that the development of diachronic aspects of cognition are far from complete at age twelve.

Montangero finds significant differences in capacity to think about the evolutive process between the lower and upper ends of the seven- to twelve-year-age range. He places the transition in this type of understanding at around the age of nine or ten. Montangero notes that the younger children in his study were definitely interested in change and that they understood that time and change are correlated. He also found that they possessed theories concerning the causes and chronology of different types of changes. Although they could recognize transformations in time, they did not exhibit the ability to imagine transformations based on these criteria. In terms of transformational schemes, he found that for this younger group, they were largely quantitative and external in nature. Montangero observed that the greatest difference between children in the younger and older groups he studied was in the area of causal explanations. While younger children clearly showed the ability to think about causality, they couldn't do so when the stages of transformation were numerous. What he found in such cases was that the children were more likely to attribute a transformation to some event in the present rather than link it to a preceding state. Montangero compares the state of diachronic thinking for children aged seven to nine to that of a series of photographs taken at regular intervals. He says that transformations in time for this age group are much like a series of static snapshots rather than a process of change, which might be more analogous to a moving picture. Montangero is not denying that the younger children have the capacity to understand change or to think across time. He is, however, saying that this capacity is limited, particularly in linking stages of transformation for the purpose of generating causal explanations and in recognizing qualitative types of changes.

Montangero says that the way in which evolutive processes are imagined, and the ability to link present with past or future states, changes dramatically around the age of ten. He sees preadolescents as being infinitely more capable of decentering themselves from the present than are younger children and more adept at recognizing the interconnectedness between states. The critical piece of Montangero's work is the way in which he interprets this development. He contends that this transformation in conceptualizing change occurs not because of knowledge acquisition, but that it is due to the reorganization or restructuring of a child's knowledge. The transition, he says, is attributed to both brain maturity and influences within the environment.

A review of Montangero's work is relevant to the teaching of history because it raises questions regarding the way children construct narratives of the human past. While he makes no attempt to link the diachronic approach to what has been called historical thinking, the implications seem apparent. He points to the importance of the diachronic process in conceptualizing transformation and change in the physical world, but it seems that these same principles might also be important in understanding the way children construct social phenomena and the way they link action and events across time.

The Interpretive Act

There was a child went forth every day,
And the first object he looked upon, that object he became,
And that object became part of him for the day or a certain part
of the day,
Or for many years or stretching cycles of years.
    Walt Whitman (1959:138)

Conceptualizing the human past is more than ordering and structuring selected information bits. When we study the past, whatever our age, we are engaging in a relationship, a relationship with the objects and other kinds of evidence that are available to us. Objects or artifacts are particularly important to our understanding of the unwritten past. Whitman's words summarize beautifully and succinctly this dynamic that exists between self and the objectified world. We are, to a great extent, the things we choose to have around us and they, in turn, are us. What I mean by this, as it relates to interpreting the past, is that we do not understand objects outside of our self, our own identity. The objects or evidence of the past that we encounter are, thus, understood through the self and our interpretations of the past grow out of this blending that takes place between self and objects, or self and text.

Hermeneutics is understood to be the theory or art of interpretation (Gadamer 1981:88). It is a theory that is rooted in the notion that interpretation is culturally and historically situated. The interplay between the parts and the whole, known as the hermeneutic circle, is seen as central to the making of meaning. Another key aspect of hermeneutics is the attention paid to the interpreter and her or his influence on the interpretation. The interpreter is not outside of the interpretation; she or he is an integral part of it. Interpretation viewed from a hermeneutic frame is seen as a fusion of horizons. According to Gadamer, the term horizon refers to the range of possibilities that can be seen from a particular vantage point (1981:269).

In other words, the image that a student holds of some particular part of the past is the product of her or his experience with the available evidence and is situated in her or his personal history, this may be seen as one horizon. It is the student's vantage point. The evidence examined by the student was collected or assembled according to a specific plan, the plan may have been created by the student's teacher or in other situations, such as museum exhibits, it may have been designed by archaeologists or historians. This body of evidence both permits and limits what the student will come to know about the past. Although it does not control the student's interpretation of the past, it is another horizon and, as such, plays a role in the interpretation. The documents or artifacts that are the evidence of the past were created by individuals at another point in time and were imbued with the meaning that their creators gave them, yet another horizon. This meaning may not be accessible to those who are of another culture and another time but the student, as well as the teacher, archaeologist, and historian, constructs an understanding based on the information that is available. The meanings they derive from the objects are constructed in the present and are, of course, influenced by the orientations of those doing the interpretation. Although the student may not be cognizant of it, these various horizons come together in some fashion and influence her or his interpretation.

Hermeneutics is a theory of interpretation that focuses on understanding rather than on explaining. According to Bruner, the interpretive act is not analogous to explanation, nor does it preclude explanation. To distinguish between the two, Bruner says:

> The explanatory aims to elucidate the necessary and/or sufficient conditions that enable us to recognize a mental state. . . . The interpretive way is after-the-fact and typically context-dependent, and therefore "historical." [1996:102]

> Being interpretive does not imply being anti-empirical, anti-experimental, or even anti-quantitative. It simply means that we must first make sense of what people tell us in light of the triad (perspective, context, and discourse) before we start explaining it . . . the two (explanation and interpretation) are mutually enlightening but not reducible to each other. [1996:113]

To illustrate:

> You cannot explain a story; all you can do is give it variant interpretations. You can explain falling bodies by reference to a theory of gravity. But you can only interpret what might have happened to Sir Issac Newton when the legendary apple fell on his head in the orchard. [1996:122]

The interpretive act, as viewed from a hermeneutic frame, points to the difficulty of seeing anything beyond ourselves when we look into the past. This approach helps us understand why, in Wineburg's words, historical thinking is an unnatural act (2001). Even so, the hermeneutic paradigm also recognizes that there is the possibility for making the familiar strange. Through a conscious awareness of the fusion of horizons there is the potential to move beyond present perceptions and arrive at a new understanding. This is the challenge not only for interpreting the past but also for interpreting the present.

Summary and Concluding Comments

What do we know about learning history? The bad news is that this question has not held a prominent place among the disciplines that teach about the human past or display it in museums. The good news is that this is no longer as true as it once was and the body of information about learning history is growing. The influence of constructivism has led many disciplines to reexamine their educational beliefs and instructional methods. Although not on the forefront of this reform, history education is testing the waters and is slowly making its way into the stream. Most significant has probably been the realization that with history, as with other subjects, people have preconceived ideas that powerfully affect what they will learn. Another significant finding related to knowledge construction is that students as young as elementary age probably do have the capacity for diachronic thinking; this is an important understanding in that it changes traditional ideas about introducing history into the elementary school curricula.

Research into learning history has also enlightened our understanding of what people know about the past and what they want to know. These findings pose some interesting questions. It seems that while there are some common features regarding curiosity about the past, such as the concern with social history and practices of ordinary people, there are also differences in how people view and use the past that are related to culture and ethnicity.

The discussions of constructivisim, cognitive development, and interpretation are included in this chapter in order to place research regarding the learning of history within a more holistic frame. To ignore the importance of any of these areas would place limits on what can be learned. As Bruner states:

> Just as you cannot fully understand human action without taking account of its biological evolutionary roots and, at the same time, understanding how it is construed in the meaning making of the actors involved in it, so you cannot understand it fully without knowing how and where it is *situated*. . . . It is practically impossible to understand a thought, an act, a move of any sort apart from the situation in which it occurs. Biology and culture both operate locally: however grand the sweep of their principles, they find a final common path in the here and now: in the immediate "definition of the situation," in the immediate discourse setting, in the immanent state of the nervous system, local and situated. [1996:167]

I have chosen to consider each of these aspects of constructing the past not to dissect the question, but to reveal its complexity, to place it within its biological, social, and situational contexts. The importance of each of these areas to understanding how children construct the past is illustrated in the following discussion of my research with fourth-grade students in southwestern Colorado.

CONSTRUCTING THE PAST: A CASE STUDY FROM SOUTHWESTERN COLORADO

II

A Sense of Place

3

Southwest Colorado

IT IS DIFFICULT TO SAY WHERE THIS STORY BEGAN, but it would surely have to include the 2,000-mile road trip from Chapel Hill, North Carolina, where I was living at the time of my dissertation research in 1996, to the research setting in southwestern Colorado. It was a pilgrimage across space and in search of time, or more specifically, in search of how children construct time.

When I leave the East behind, I feel myself grow lighter with each mile. My personal preference for landscape is that of big sky and bright clear air. Although I grew up in a narrow, thickly forested valley of southern Appalachia, I feel more at home in the open expanses of plains, deserts, and high-altitude mountains that are found west of the Mississippi River. I have traveled this route many times over the last twenty-five years, sometimes by land, often by air. In either case, I always reflect on this sense of openness and the images that accompany it. I am filled with questions about landscapes, particularly how they influence us psychologically and how they carry different meanings, both personally and cross-culturally:

> It's true the landscape forms the mind.

> (JOY HARJO 1989)

> The landscape sits in the center of Pueblo belief and identity. Any narratives about the Pueblo people necessarily give a great deal of attention and detail to all aspects of a landscape.

> (LESLIE MARMON SILKO 1993)

I think the old people swirled with the place and became a part of what was there already. They extended the forms of the boulders with their own kinds of structures. They honored the springs at the canyon heads by building and planting around them. Use is honoring. They appreciated the containment of earth and sky.

(RINA SWENTZELL 1993)

I grew up among these ruins. My first awareness that a "vanished people" had once flourished here came with a school trip to Mesa Verde nearly forty-five years ago. I was six. Those first views of Cliff Palace, Balcony House, Far View, and the pots and tools in the Chapin Mesa Museum made a deep impression on me. In ensuing years I visited countless archaeological sites here. . . . My youthful view of these places was that of an incurable romantic. I simply made up stories about them; I peopled these silent villages with imaginary men, women, and children living peacefully in an idyllic pastoral world set mostly in spectacular sandstone canyons.

(IAN THOMPSON 1995)

There is probably no place in the United States where the human past, beyond a couple of centuries, is evident to the extent that it is on the Colorado Plateau and other parts of the desert Southwest. An extremely arid climate and remote location contribute to the preservation of sites that date back hundreds and, in some cases, thousands of years. As Ian Thompson's words express, it is a landscape that invites narrative. People and place in this part of the world are intimately connected. It is not a place that can tolerate a high degree of carelessness or exploitation—it is a land where balance is a necessity. As Joy Harjo and Leslie Silko point out, the landscape is a part of the people and part of their beliefs, or in Rina Swentzell's words, "the old people swirled with the place and became a part of what was there already." And so, to talk about children from the present and their view of the Pueblo past, it is essential to also talk about the land that is common to both.

When I arrived in early autumn to begin this research project, the hills around Waterville, Colorado, were a scarlet blaze. The gamble oak that prevails on the thin rocky soil at this elevation was uncharacteristically colorful. In most years, the leaves change from a dull lack-luster green to a dull lack-luster brown; some nuance in the precipitation and temperature norms had, in that particular year, resulted in a breathtaking spectacle, and I felt privileged to be in the right place at the right time. Stories of going "into the field" often commence with hardship and inconvenience. My experience was quite the contrary. The only difficulty I found in this setting was the lure of the outdoors. It was a challenge to stay on task when groves of aspen were forming such riotous displays of gold among the spruces and firs. During my stay in this place of awful beauty, I witnessed winter's first snowfalls and began to understand just how different life in southwestern Colorado is from that of piedmont North Carolina. I was amazed to find that, at 7:00 AM, with about four inches of snow on the ground, school buses were running as usual and kids along the route were seemingly oblivious to the change in weather. I suppose that snow takes on a different meaning for a ten-year-old when it does not have the power to close schools.

My research actually took place in two different communities in southwestern Colorado: the town of Waterville, where the participating schools are located, and the area surrounding Crow Canyon Archaeological Center, where these classes were engaged in a two-day field experience. The communities are different in a number of ways but most noticeably in geography. On the Colorado Plateau, it is possible to experience the solitude of desert canyons and the thin air of high mountains in the same afternoon. The town of Waterville experiences rain on an almost daily basis in the late summer months and can have snowfalls of a foot or more in winter. The area around Crow Canyon, with only fourteen inches of precipitation annually, could be considered semi-desert. Eight hundred years ago, Pueblo people farmed the broad flat mesa tops around Crow Canyon, as well as the moist canyon bottoms. Anglo farmers till the same soil today, relying on extensive irrigation systems, unlike the Pueblo people who were dry-land farmers.

Waterville is 6,500 feet in elevation and the growing season is relatively short, making it a precarious choice for farming now, just as it would have been 800 years ago. I have always found it interesting that mountain towns display their elevation so prominently; it is seemingly a source of pride. People living between sea level and 1,000 feet can rarely give the exact elevation of their community but everyone in a mountain town will know and will provide this fact as one of the first bits of local information for outsiders. It is an important fact, for elevations of this extreme have an effect on a great many things, including human endurance, automobile performance, and the temperature at which water boils or cakes bake.

Waterville is a fairly large town by Western standards. Population figures vary depending on the source, but 1990 census figures place the population for the town itself at 12,430 and 32,284 for the county (by 1999, the population estimate for the town had grown to almost 14,000 and over 43,000 for the county). The town's population has, historically, been somewhat erratic due to economic ties to the oil, gas, and mining industries. In the last thirty years, however, Waterville has experienced a steady growth due, in part, to a booming tourist trade. A breakdown of population by race and ethnicity is problematic because of the way these categories have been constructed on census forms. Hispanic, Native American, and Asian peoples are sometimes counted as white and sometimes as other. A rough estimate would place racial and ethnic minority groups at about 12–20 percent of the general population. Even though the population of Waterville might be described as predominantly white, it typifies the population of the state of Colorado as well as many of the other states in the Rocky Mountain West.

One might expect a high population of Pueblo people in the area due to their deep history in the region. However, the migration that led them out of the area in the late 1200s was a journey for keeps. According to archaeologists, the region was basically unoccupied from around A.D. 1300 until the Utes and Paiutes began moving in from the deserts of southern Nevada and southeastern California, and the Navajos and Apaches from the forests of northern Canada (Brown 1995). Each of the groups brought with them their own lifeways and they related to the landscape differently. The Navajo developed a pastoral way of life centered around herds of sheep, while the Utes continued to move in bands as hunters and gatherers up until the 1800s when they were forced onto reservations.

The first Europeans to begin moving through the Southwest were Spaniards who came north from Mexico as early as the 1500s. Their presence was not felt in Colorado as significantly as it was farther south in New Mexico and Arizona. European settlement was negligible in southwest Colorado until the late 1800s when a railway system and the promise of riches in the way of gold and silver lured them into the area. The Great Cut Dike Irrigation project attracted settlers to the agricultural lands around the Crow Canyon Archaeological Center (Connolly 1996). The Anglo population has steadily increased throughout the area over the last hundred years and is now the majority population in the vicinity of Crow Canyon as well as in the town of Waterville.

The human-built landscape in southwest Colorado is truly a mixed bag. The area's kaleidoscope of race, class, culture, and history has resulted in an unusual, and sometimes confusing, assemblage of symbols and signs. Within a few miles of Waterville, one can rent horses for trail rides; experience a cowboy chuckwagon dinner; go skiing, biking, hiking, and rafting; take helicopter rides; tour an archaeological site; visit galleries selling works created by Navajo, Pueblo, and Ute artists; catch fish; swim; play golf; buy hand-crafted furniture made from aspen logs; witness a melodrama; go for a ride on a narrow-gauge railroad; hunt elk and mule deer; take in a college lecture series; see Indian dances; and attend music festivals that run the gamut from bluegrass to Bach. The term "Indian" is an ambiguous construct in general, but it is certainly so in this region. It is represented by "Anasazi" ruins, frybread, turquoise, pottery, rugs, silver jewelry, and beadwork, as well as fake teepees and giant arrows poised outside of tourist shops.

During one of my first visits into the project schools, I asked the students to help me develop a concept map of Waterville life. There was a dual purpose embedded in this task; it provided a way to teach the students how to construct their own concept maps that I would need later in the research project and it taught me a great deal about how these youngsters view their own town (for a more detailed discussion of concept maps, see chapter 9). The clear message I got from them is that southern Colorado is about the outdoors and that activity is centered around outdoor recreation. They knew an extensive amount about the area and were eager to educate me. They told me about the major industries, which were, according to them, the making of chocolate and outdoor wear. They identified the river and the train as being emblematic of Waterville. The children were particularly aware of the natural environment, giving great detail regarding seasonal changes, and they told me a lot about the flora and fauna of the area. From my experience, the same age students from the more densely settled East Coast do not generally exhibit this degree of knowledge of, or attention to, the natural world. I believe Waterville students know the outdoors so well because they spend a lot of time there. When they spoke of recreation, it was generally in the context of family activities, which were almost always situated outdoors. In discussing this with other Colorado residents who are former easterners, they explained that, "People play here more than they do in the East."

The Waterville students also had an interesting perspective on local culture. When they developed the "people" strand of their concept map, the first category they came up with was not tourists, as I had expected, but "hippies." When we speak of groups of people, we often frame the discussion in differences—we talk first about those who are not like us, or are not mainstream. The fourth graders in Waterville could easily see this young counterculture of dreadlocks and tie-dye as being characteristic of town life but unlike the majority of people residing there.

A fair-sized undergraduate college is located in Waterville, which accounts, in part, for the prevalence of a large young adult population. But it does not completely explain the look of this group that seems locked in a time warp, their clocks seemingly stalled out sometime around 1969. In this way, Waterville is not unlike many other historic mining towns in the southern Colorado Rockies. Many of these towns, Telluride for example, experienced a rebirth in the 1960s and 1970s when a number of original hippies began to settle in some of the older houses that were built during the mining boom at the turn of the last century. A great many of these older homes were in a state of disrepair and could be had for, as they say, a song. Waterville and some of the other former mining towns are again experiencing a cultural shift. The old Victorian houses are now becoming upscale properties; pricey ski and golf resorts have been built on the outskirts of town; and a new breed of trendy shops and restaurants have opened up to accommodate the more expensive tastes of moneyed newcomers.

Surprisingly, the students said little about the constant flow of tourists through the area and they also failed to mention the cowboy culture that is highly visible in this eclectic community. This is particularly remarkable in light of the fact that Waterville was holding a cowboy-poetry gathering during my first week in the schools. Several of the poets made presentations dressed in full regalia, including chaps, hats, kerchiefs, and boots. If I had mentioned either the tourists or the cowboy influence, the students would have likely included them on the concept map. I believe these groups were omitted from the concept maps because the students either did not consider them to be a significant aspect of Waterville life or because they are so common that they have achieved a taken-for-granted status in the community.

The Schools

Two primary criteria guided my selection of schools for the research project. First, I realized that I needed to escape the traditional model for teaching history in school. If I expected to learn about ways young people construct the past and how educational experiences might contribute to the construction, I realized that I needed to examine a place, or places, where this actually occurs. Thus, I decided it would be critical to locate the project in an educationally rich setting in order to maximize opportunities for observing students who were genuinely engaged in studies of the human past. I was particularly interested in selecting classrooms that use multiple approaches in studying the past and that involve students in activities that move them beyond written text to search for human history. It seemed to me that elementary and middle school teachers would probably have greater freedom to design these more active and engaging programs than those who teach in high schools. Many structural aspects of high schools, such as the departmentalization of subject matter, the fragmentation of the school day, and punitive accountability systems, work to inhibit innovation.

Second, I recognized that the study must focus on an area of history that has not yet become a mainstream, regularized part of the curriculum but, rather, one that necessitates a more creative approach to instruction. I decided to situate the research project in classrooms that were studying a Native American past because Native peoples have a deeper history in North America than anyone else and it might be said that their past is also the most excluded. Most states have a Native American Heritage week or month but these are rarely acknowledged in the same way as Black History Month. In trying to understand how students were constructing a Native American past, I would not have to be as concerned with instructional materials that alienate students. The teaching of Indian history has not yet been reduced to the routinized type of study that seems to prevail in traditional history classes. Indian history, ironically, usually appears in the classroom around Thanksgiving or in the first chapter of an American History text, where 12,000 years get compressed into a brief account of the land bridge crossing and contact with Europeans. Any mention thereafter is often in the context of white history in America. I felt that if I could find classrooms where an in-depth study of Indian history was taking place, I would be more likely to witness a richer teaching of the past and find students who were not tuned-out.

A number of more specific characteristics also influenced site selection for this project: the type of classroom, the instructor, and the curriculum being taught. It was important to locate the project within public schools because enrollment for private institutions is often less diverse in terms of race, class, and ethnicity. A public school setting was also important for diversifying the study population in terms of academic performance; private institutions are sometimes more homogeneous in this respect. Teachers were another consideration. As with all of these categories, I developed a list of ideals and then sought to match the list as closely as possible with real people. My aim was to identify teachers who were committed to having lively classes and interested students. I was also seeking teachers who truly enjoy history and cultural studies and who are reflective in their practice. Such teachers would, I felt, become actively involved in the project and contribute as members of a research team. Finally, I wanted to conduct the project in the context of a history unit that was multi-vocal in nature and utilized textbooks only as references.

I looked to the Crow Canyon Archaeological Center for assistance in identifying project schools because I was already familiar with their curriculum, teaching philosophy, and staff. I knew that they were interested in issues related to learning and assessment. Crow Canyon's location, 2,000 miles from my home, introduced obvious difficulties such as increasing the cost of the project and limiting on-going communication with project participants after the initial data-collection phase. However, the benefits of starting out as, at least, a semi-insider far outweighed the difficulties. Crow Canyon offered support in several ways; particularly critical was their help in identifying the schools and teachers that would be bringing classes to their facility during the time frame laid out for the project.

The staff at Crow Canyon was able to connect me with two Waterville elementary schools, Dixon and South, whose fourth-grade classes would be participating in the Center's two-day education program. Each of these schools had a history of bringing their students to Crow Canyon, and I found the principals of these schools to be highly supportive of the Center's work. While I had envisioned having no more than fifty or sixty students in the study, I soon realized that this would not be the case. The principals of both schools indicated that, although they gave their own approval for the research project, I needed to seek consent from the fourth-grade teachers—all five of them. The teachers at the two schools were intrigued by the project, so I found myself working with not 50, but 110 fourth-grade students. This figure is an approximation; class enrollments varied somewhat during the data-collection period and a few of the students did not participate in the field trip to Crow Canyon. In reality, it would have been difficult to work with only one class from each school because classes were mixed for the Crow Canyon trip. For example, the three classes from Dixon were divided into only two groups for the field experience.

Dixon and South are, at their core, one-story brick structures and, at the time of my research, both schools had been recently renovated or had additions built onto the existing structures. Dixon and South elementary schools both fall under the administration of the Waterville school district and, thus, share much in common, but each also exhibits its own unique flavor. Although schools are subject to a variety of influences, I would attribute the major differences between the two schools to the nature of the communities that they draw students from and to school-level leadership. The schools are within a few miles of one another and had comparable enrollments at the time the project was conducted (380 at Dixon and 300 at South). Their mission statements were also fairly similar:

> *Dixon Elementary* strives to provide an enjoyable, challenging, and relevant learning environment where students will experience immediate success and develop the knowledge and skills necessary for continuing social and physical growth, and academic achievement.

> It is the purpose of *South School* to provide a learning environment that integrates sound social, emotional, and physical health with academic goals and prepares students for change, social interaction, and problem solving.

Both schools were interested in enhancing the self-esteem of their students and ensuring that they all felt successful. They also emphasized citizenship and the importance of preparing students for participation in the world in which they live.

Attendance at several schoolwide events influenced my view of Dixon. During my stay in Waterville, I attended a spaghetti dinner held at Dixon to raise money for the trip to Crow Canyon, I accompanied the fourth graders on an environmental studies field trip, and attended an assembly program. If such programs were held at South while I was conducting this research project, I was unaware of them. Both schools have bright interiors and project a sense of warmth and hospitality. South and Dixon are both located in heavy residential areas of Waterville, and many students ride bikes or walk to school. All the classrooms involved in the project had five or six computers each, but I rarely saw students completing assignments on them.

Dixon's principal, Dan Stone, was openly supportive of the study and continually made inquiries regarding its progress. He obviously enjoys working with kids and seems to know each one by name. They are, in turn, comfortable with him and, I believe, see him as approachable and pleasant. He accompanied one of the Dixon groups to Crow Canyon where he fulfilled routine chaperone tasks and prepared a bonfire/marshmallow roast for the students. South's principal, Lynda Collins, seemed far less visible in her school, but this perspective could be related to the time of day when I was present in the classrooms. My only conversation with her was via telephone, except for a brief introduction when she came into one of the classrooms I was working in. While open to the project, she never asked me about its progress, as did the principal at Dixon.

The educational programs of the two schools were similar and, as they belong to the same school district, reflected similar curricula and philosophy. Both included whole language as part of the language arts program but incorporated other methods and approaches, including instruction in phonics. In the area of mathematics, Dixon's course of study seemed focused more on skills, where South's was more process oriented and used a hands-on approach. Social Studies in both schools was integrated with other disciplines through a thematic approach.

I had difficulty gaining insight into the kind of image South elementary hoped to project, but it was quite clear that Dixon was working toward becoming a true community school, complete with high parent involvement and community partnerships. According to their home page on the Internet:

> In an effort to re-establish Dixon as a neighborhood school, a variety of events and activities occurred that brought the Dixon community into the school and also put the Dixon students out into the community. This outreach effort helped create a more open, welcoming family-oriented educational environment.

The presence of family was certainly felt during the spaghetti dinner I attended at Dixon; it seemed as if the entire school community was present, and the event garnered more than $5,000, far more than was needed to take the fourth graders to Crow Canyon. South's funds for Crow Canyon were acquired through the ingenuity of one of the teachers who sought out local businesses to sponsor the trip. Dixon and South both had a number of special opportunities and activities for students including an after-school program, Odyssey of the Mind, Knowledge Bowl, orchestra, art, music, and community service projects.

The Crow Canyon Archaeological Center

The Crow Canyon Archaeological Center was officially formed in 1983 as a not-for-profit organization. The Center's mission is to initiate and conduct archaeological research and public education programs in partnership with Native Americans and institutions with common interests. The archaeological research focus for the institution is the ancestral Pueblo (Anasazi) occupation in the Mesa Verde region. The Center has developed a high standard of research and scholarship and offers an established program that enables lay people to participate with professional archaeologists in carrying out scientific research. Each year, about 3,500 students and adults participate in the Center's programs. Tuitions, donations, grants, and memberships fund the organization's activities.

The Center's student population ranges in age from nine or ten to adult. Crow Canyon Archaeological Center rests on the belief that in-depth learning experiences and the publication of research results make a difference in public archaeology. The Center has received a number of prestigious awards for contributing to heritage education and preservation, including the Presidential Award for Historic Preservation and the Society for American Archaeology's award for Excellence in Public Education.

Crow Canyon's 110-acre campus is nestled in a small valley surrounded by native pinyon-juniper woodland (since the time of the research project, the Center has acquired additional land and the campus now consists of 170 acres). The main campus building houses classrooms, an education lab used for simulated excavations, archaeological research laboratories, a temporary curation room, and staff offices. The Crow Canyon lodge consists of a dining hall and dormitory-style housing for seventy students. There is also a large patio on the east side of the building where people naturally come together, making it the hub of campus life. The influence of pueblo architecture is apparent in these buildings; they have flat rooflines and stucco exteriors that resemble adobe. The lodge also has a large prominent window that is patterned after the T-shaped doorways found in some ancient pueblos. A large meadow provides play areas for children, including dirt basketball and volleyball courts. A nature trail winds through the pinyon-juniper woodland.

The archaeological sites studied by the Center's staff are not located on the campus itself but are at various locations nearby. Many of these are on public lands or property belonging to the Archaeological Conservancy. The Center occasionally conducts research on private land. At the time I was conducting this study, the Center was excavating at Yellow Jacket Pueblo, the largest ancestral Pueblo site in the Mesa Verde region. Because the site is located in the open and has been exposed to various kinds of natural and human impacts over the last 700 years, it is a ruin in the literal sense. There are no standing walls but there are deep depressions where pit structures were located and row upon row of high rubble mounds where above-ground buildings once stood. Because the area was occupied for a long period of time and by a large number of people, it also contains deep midden areas filled with pottery sherds, ash, chipped stone, and various other objects that were part of daily life for the people who once lived there. Although there are no standing structures, Yellow Jacket is an impressive site, even for youngsters, because it is so extensive and because the evidence of the past is so highly visible.

Closing Thoughts

I agree with Harjo's assertion that landscape has a powerful effect on the mind. All of our thoughts and actions are situated within particular landscapes. Because of this, I have tried to portray the multiple settings that were important to this research project: the schools, the Crow Canyon Archaeological Center, Yellowjacket Pueblo, the town of Waterville, and the natural landscape of southwest Colorado. The ways in which students in the project constructed Pueblo history, as well as my interpretations of their constructions, were and are affected by each of the landscapes described in this chapter. The discussion of each of these locations is meant to provide a context for the reader so that he or she can better construct his or her own meaning regarding the project.

The Research Design and Project Parameters: 4
Teachers, Students, and Curriculum

I have long argued that explaining what children do is not enough; the new agenda is to determine what they think they are doing and what their reasons are for doing it.

(JEROME BRUNER 1996:49)

We must place ourselves inside the heads of our students and try to understand as far as possible the sources and strengths of their conceptions.

(HOWARD GARDNER 1991:253)

A Question of Approach

RESEARCH METHODS ARE LARGELY DETERMINED by the nature of the questions being asked. However, I think it is worth arguing that we select or pose questions that fit our personally preferred methods of discovery. In some fashion, our understanding of the nature of investigation contributes to the construction of our research questions. In the end, it probably doesn't matter whether the question defines the approach or the approach structures the question; this is chicken-and-egg logic. What is important is to not let a particular methodological orientation limit what might be learned. My research in southwest Colorado was informed by findings from both qualitative and quantitative studies. Large-scale quantitative studies that have identified the difficulties with K–12 history helped me understand the extent of these problems and the significance of the question that I was posing. Qualitative projects that addressed the learning of history, although scarce, were of enormous value in helping me refine my research question and develop strategies for investigation.

The challenge I faced in this study was to understand the problem from the inside. Another challenge was to examine the process of conceptual development—to trace the movement of understanding, rather than to simply look for learning outcomes. I wanted to understand *what* meaning students made of the past and to understand *how* those meanings were made. It was the *process* for constructing meaning that I wanted to explore, and I determined that a qualitative approach was the most useful for an investigation of this nature: "Qualitative inquiry is highly appropriate in studying process because depicting process requires detailed description; the experience of process typically varies for different people; process is fluid and dynamic; and participants' perceptions are a key process consideration" (Patton 1990:95).

Certain aspects of the problems with history education, such as the quality of textbooks and instruction, have been examined, but what happens in the minds of students when they think about the human past is largely unexplored. It seems inconceivable that so obvious a source of information should be so overwhelmingly ignored. Yet, in light of behaviorist approaches to educational research, it is probably not so amazing. This is not to say that youth have not been involved in research; they have been watched, tested, quizzed, surveyed, analyzed, categorized, and labeled—they have been the objects of educational research. They have been talked *about* at length, but talked *to* very little. Even in studies of cognitive development where children have been questioned at length, this questioning has seldom valued children as consultants or informants; they have simply been expected to answer more questions for an authoritative adult. Apparently, it has not seemed necessary to let them in on the purpose for the questioning. This position assumes that children either cannot reflect on their own thinking or that they cannot express their thoughts. Perhaps it assumes both; I think that neither of these positions is true.

To illustrate, when a second grader demonstrates mathematical skills that are many years beyond the level at which he has been instructed, a good teacher will ask, "How did you get that?" The child will likely talk through the solution and the teacher will be satisfied. She or he may assume that the skill was learned from an older sibling or that the child's parents are providing accelerated instruction at home. The exceptional teacher will, however, continue to quiz the child and ask, "Where did you learn how to do that?" This situation was played out in the classroom of a former colleague. When she raised that second question, "Where did you learn how to do that?" she discovered that she was working with a child who was, literally, discovering mathematics for himself. As we continued to work with him over the next months, he was given standardized tests that indicated he was exceptionally advanced in mathematics—but we knew that. The truly important things we learned about this seven-year-old's thinking were the things he told us.

We learned that he developed many of his theories regarding numbers while pour-ing over his vast collection of baseball cards. His mother confessed that he often won the family baseball pool he participated in with his older brother, father, un-cles, and cousins. I am awed to think of all that we miss in education by assum-ing that children do not, or can not, reflect on their own thought processes.

The objectified, exotic "others" of educational research are children. In as-suming we can learn nothing from them, we ensure that this is the case. I am, for-tunately, not alone in this belief. There are certainly others who believe we can learn from youth by being explicit about our questions rather than devising elab-orate instruments to trick the information from them or by watching them from afar. Historically, ethnographers have been guilty of the same exclusive approach in their studies. In the last couple of decades, the field of anthropology has scorned these methods. Criticism of the approach is interesting; practitioners are charged with the allegation that they are treating their informants "like children."

The point I want to stress here is the important role that children played in this research project. In qualitative studies, data may be gathered from various types of observations, document review, interviews, and surveys; it is not a re-quirement of qualitative design to include participants or informants as members of the research team. It is just as possible to exclude voices other than the re-searcher's in qualitative studies as it is in quantitative projects. I would like to say that the children were at the center of this project, but it would be more accurate to say they occupied that position along with me. I formulated the guiding ques-tion and directed the project. It would be dishonest to me and to the study to im-ply that my hand was not heavy in the process. However, I would like to believe, and it was my intention, that once the project began, the children who participated charted the course we took. I would also place a few other adults at this center, particularly the classroom teachers with whom I worked.

The Data

Methods in qualitative research are oriented toward exploration, discovery, and in-ductive logic. The particular research methods chosen, or data-collection strategies used, are situation specific. Appropriate methods reflect the interplay between re-sources, possibilities, creativity, and personal judgment. As Michael Patton says, "Qualitative research, like diplomacy, is the art of the possible" (1990:13). Who will be using the information, what kind of information is needed, how that in-formation will be used, and what resources are available always have influence on the guiding questions.

In qualitative studies, questions and approach are open ended in nature to help the researcher see the world in terms of the respondents. With an open-ended approach, study participants have greater opportunity to show depth of emotion and the ways that they organize their knowledge. The particular type of question determines, to a great extent, the most appropriate mode of data collection. Questions asking: "What?" or "How many?" can be addressed through surveys or questionnaires. "How?" and "Why?" questions are better explored through more in-depth approaches such as interviews, focus groups, and case studies.

With these guidelines in mind, I mapped out my strategy for data collection—I decided I would look at everything. There were obvious problems with this course of action, not the least of which was the ill fit between the proposed and the possible. But, because the territory I sought to explore was so extensively unknown, I believed that everything connected with it might be considered data. I determined that the only reasonable action would be to locate myself within the classrooms as much as time and resources would allow. In reality, this turned out to be approximately six consecutive weeks.

I was in classrooms with students for an average of five hours per day. In some cases, particularly during the visits to Crow Canyon, my days were much longer, usually closer to ten hours. Although this was a significant chunk of time, I always felt that it was never enough because my attention was split between the two schools. Fortunately, they are located within a few miles of one another and the switch between the two gave me time for lunch and writing field notes. I tried to vary the time of day I was in the schools to get a feel for their regular schedule and to have some time at the end of the day to talk informally with teacher participants. During the six weeks of fieldwork, I managed to temper my desire for collecting everything with a pragmatic sense of what I could reasonably manage. In addition to the naturalistic data, I also constructed three specific tasks that were intended to elicit information in a more direct way: concept maps, one-on-one interviews with a selected group of students, and a follow-up survey. These are explained in greater detail in sections that follow; a general list of the types of data collected appears in appendix I.

The Research Team

The Classroom Teachers

One of the most important lessons I learned during my fourteen years in public schools was that there are many different ways to teach and many teaching styles that are equally effective. The five classrooms involved in this study had much in common but each one also had its own unique character. Each teacher approached the study of Pueblo history in different ways and, except for the common experiences each class had at Crow Canyon, instruction varied greatly. As is typical in any elementary school, the majority of teachers were women (four out of five).

Four of the five might be considered veteran teachers—three of the five actually had more than twenty-five years of teaching experience each—and one teacher was beginning his first year in the classroom. In this section, I hope to build a more vivid picture of each of the teachers and his/her class. Three of these summaries include self-reflection from the teachers regarding their students and instruction. Although each teacher was encouraged to contribute such information, I received only three responses. Because I was only in each of these classrooms for a brief time period, I felt that I could not characterize them as effectively as the teachers themselves could. Where those perspectives are missing, I rely on my own observations, field notes, and other data to portray the classes.

The teacher portraits that follow are largely positive but this is not to say that I viewed all instruction in a positive light. However, a commentary on, and analysis of, instruction is not what this project was about. The teachers who participated did so with the understanding that we were trying to look at student constructs, not teacher performance. A critique of their teaching or their instructional programs would betray a trust and move beyond the boundaries of our negotiated relationship.

I begin this discussion of teachers and their classes with Caroline Norton, a thoughtful woman who was teaching fourth grade at South Elementary.

CAROLINE NORTON I found that I had much in common with Caroline, we had each taught for about fourteen years and we were near the same age. The first time I met Caroline was on a beautiful autumn day; the sidewalk that runs past Waterville's South Elementary was a carpet of aspen gold. School had just been dismissed for the day, and I found Caroline in her classroom with a group of students who had not yet left for home. Caroline's classroom reflected the warmth of the day, both in temperature and in spirit. She was taking care of last-minute questions from students, chatting with a parent, and closing down the school day. Her soft voice and patient attitude brought to mind other teachers I had worked with. As she elicited help from students to take care of clean-up tasks, I could sense a mutual respect. After the classroom had cleared, I spent the next several minutes shadowing Caroline as she responded to all the errands and messages she had received during the day. As we traveled from classroom, to office, to workroom, Caroline introduced me to everyone we encountered. While we walked she told me of the fund-raising project she conducted to make the Crow Canyon trip possible. To other outsiders, this level of activity would have seemed exhausting, for me it was a reminder of life in an elementary school.

Caroline and I met for two hours of planning during this first visit. I found her highly organized and thoughtful in her approach to teaching. She showed me the scope and sequence for the unit she would teach on Pueblo history and provided a

copy of her schedule so I could be present during instruction. She gave me extensive information about her students and their capabilities as well as some of their
limitations. It was clear to me that Caroline is a highly professional teacher who
takes her work seriously and aims for quality instruction in her classroom; she reflects on her practice and she worries about getting it right. The following is Caroline's assessment of her class.

> As a whole, I see my class as very eager to learn and, as with most kids, they love
> the hands-on involvement in activities. They do well in class discussions, but also
> need help and modeling with some types of higher-level thinking. Out of twenty-
> one students, almost half of them have qualified or have been considered for our
> Independent Study program (gifted and talented). At the other end academically,
> there are four students who read at least two years below grade level. This class is
> fun to brainstorm ideas with because they bring up things I wouldn't think of and
> are very creative. A majority of them also love art.
>
> As far as my teaching style, I realize the importance of identifying each stu-
> dent's learning style, their strengths and the areas they need to work on. In doing
> so, I can build on their strengths and help them identify and set goals in what they
> need to achieve during the year. I work on building respect between the students
> and discussing how we all have strengths and weaknesses and that we're here to en-
> courage each other. I also believe it is important to provide a lot of different ac-
> tivities and choices. We do large group activities and discussions, small group work
> and sometimes they work in partners, sometimes they work alone, sometimes I
> group students together, sometimes they choose. I feel it is my role as a teacher to
> help encourage them to become independent learners. Of course, I'm learning all
> the time, too, and adjust when I feel that I'm not meeting my goals.

SUSAN COLE Of the three fourth-grade teachers from Dixon, Susan was the
only one not planning to retire at the end of the school year. Susan's easy-going
and pleasant demeanor contribute to a strong feeling of community in her classroom. I believe her students would have described their classroom as a fun place
to be. Susan is a teacher who is not afraid to make learning active or to venture
beyond the textbook. I have great respect and admiration for teachers who have
been practicing for many years and who do not succumb to routine and repetition.
Susan had taught for more than twenty-five years at the time this study was conducted, yet she continued to experiment with her curriculum and revise her approach. She is a teacher who expects her students to think.

> It is very difficult to describe my class other than they are an interesting, chal-
> lenging, and an academically varied group of children. I have a few top students,
> a large group of average students and, as usual, a few low students. They love to
> please and like to be treated with respect and fairness. Most of them have a de-
> sire to be a leader but are unsure of what it takes. If I say something, they will re-

peat it as if it is a fact. Thus, I try to have them come up with how they feel about something rather than me stating my opinion.

I engage them in learning, help them take their learning to a higher level, and show them that learning is a lifelong endeavor. Personally, I feel by the time most of them have reached fourth grade they have the basics of academics and it is time to see how these things fit together with real life. The Crow Canyon trip is an excellent way to teach past Indian culture. The educational facilitators provide the content and allow the students to explore what they have learned with hands-on activities. Taking what they have discovered at Crow Canyon, I then try to have them solve problems and think critically about how our present day culture is related to ancient civilizations. I see directed self-discovery as the prime method of lifetime learning. Lastly, it is important that children see that learning is their job and a means to an end.

The hours I spent in Susan's classroom provided the opportunity to observe the connection between Susan's theory and her practice. I would say it is a tight fit. Susan is a teacher who has a clear understanding of what it means to learn and what the teacher's role should be in that process.

MICHAEL ORTIZ During the project period, Michael was just beginning his teaching career. He had originally chosen to enter the world of business but, after a few years, realized he was more interested in working with kids and returned to the university for a degree in education. Michael's classroom was located at South elementary, just two doors down from Caroline's. Of the five teachers involved in the project, I found Michael's approach to instruction to be the most unique. This surprised me, as many novices seek to emulate the more experienced teachers in their schools. As I reflect on this, I believe that Michael entered his first year of teaching with something that many teachers are years in developing—a personal theory of teaching and learning. During one of my first visits to his class, I found him reading Hemingway's *The Old Man and the Sea* to his students. At first, I was not sure they were listening but, as he stopped at intervals and questioned them, I became satisfied that they were. During that early visit, I learned that the class was finishing up a unit of study on John F. Kennedy and that in science they had been learning about the skeletal system. In each of these areas, it seemed as if the students had developed a rich understanding of concepts, mastered the content, and had become thoroughly excited and engaged in their studies. The other feature of Michael's classroom that caught my attention was his commitment to problem solving and critical thinking. It was not uncommon to see Michael pause from his reading and pose higher-order questions to the class that would keep them involved in discussion for great lengths of time. I got the impression that he wanted students to know that he valued their opinion and that he expected them to have one. Regarding the group, Michael said:

> The class is very diverse socially as well as economically. On one end of the spectrum, I have one student who is the child of a professor and another who is the child of a doctor. While on the other end, there are a few children of whom I am sure their parents are receiving some type of federal or state assistance. And those children do come from single-parent households. Those are the extremes. Everyone else seems to fall in the middle somewhere. The parents are very concerned with their children's education, and there is a lot of parent involvement in the class. Unfortunately, the children who are on the negative end of the spectrum don't have much parent involvement. I don't think this is much of a coincidence. However, the class as a whole works out very well. Every one gets along well with one another. This is something that we started working on in the beginning of the year, with team-building exercises and discussions about teamwork. Of course, we sometimes need refresher courses but, as a whole, they work very well together. I guess you can say that the whole is greater than the sum of its parts. They are a very intelligent class. I like the way they have blended together with each student taking a certain role. Some have taken roles as leaders while the others work to keep up to the same high standards. And, this is something that I expect them to do. I expect quite a bit from all my students. Part of my philosophy on teaching is to not teach to the lowest common denominator. I think that if you expect good things from the children, and have very high expectations, then they'll feel good about themselves and do good work. They will meet or exceed what they thought they could do.

Just as I was impressed by a teacher like Susan who had taught for many years and is always developing new ideas, I was also impressed by this first-year teacher who held such clear, positive views of children and learning. Michael also treated his students as if he believed they were smart, he even called them his "Einsteins." This was something he worked at on a daily basis, and it seemed clear that he saw this as an important part of their group identity.

BETTY HARRIS (Betty Harris did not provide me with a discussion of her students or her views on teaching. Thus, the following reflects my own observations.)

Of all the teachers participating in this project, I would describe Betty as being the most traditional in approach. Although she exercised a great deal of autonomy in deciding what she would teach, her instructional methods and classroom management seemed fairly conservative. This is probably not an entirely accurate assessment, as Betty has been spearheading the Crow Canyon field trips for a number of years—overnight field trips for fourth-grade students would not be considered a traditional teaching strategy.

It also seemed to me that, more than any of the other teachers, Betty loves history and she openly expressed a deep appreciation for the past. It was not, however, the Pueblo past that seemed to capture Betty's interest, but the past of her town and her family. The story she told me of how her family came to be in the Rocky Mountains of southern Colorado was fascinating and she was a skilled storyteller, animated and expressive. Betty's love of history was evident at other times as well. When students brought in family or personal artifacts to share with the class, it was apparent that some of the items—those of greater antiquity—captured Betty's attention. Her questions and the manner in which she examined the items reflected more than a passing interest.

When I told students of my experience with Hurricane Fran in North Carolina, Betty pointed out to the students that we often mark the passing of time with these dramatic weather events that we encounter in our lives. She gave several examples from her own childhood.

JEAN LOGAN (Jean did not provide a written account of her own perspective regarding her students; the following are my own observations.)

Jean, like the other teachers, also had her own unique style. Most significant in my mind was the sensitivity she showed in issues related to culture or diversity. She and her husband had, through the years, formed friendships with a number of Native people in the Four Corners and she seemed to be particularly knowledgeable regarding Native beliefs and customs. Jean was also very concerned with making accommodations for students with special needs. Some of the activities I conducted with her class were a little difficult for some students; in these situations, Jean sat with them and gave them personal assistance.

The composition of Jean's classroom was similar to that of Betty's and Susan's. The majority of students seemed to fall within the range that could be described as average, with a few advanced students and a few who exhibited special learning needs.

The Students

Because I was seeking to understand student constructions of the past, it was essential to form a research partnership with the students that was comfortable for both of us. Children in public schools are accustomed to seeing a number of teacher-like adults swing in and out of their classroom doors daily; they are visited by guidance counselors, special educators, student teachers, music and art teachers, school administrators, etc. I often wonder if students experience a sense of frustration or confusion with all of this coming and going or if they are able to organize and make sense of all the adults who enter into their school day. I felt it was important for the students to have an understanding of my role in their classroom and to feel at ease with me. I did not want to be a fly-on-the-wall who observes from a distance and never interacts, I wanted them to help me understand what they were thinking and I could not do this if we could not easily talk with one another. Thus, my first visits to the schools were focused on social goals.

Each teacher allowed me approximately thirty minutes of class time to introduce myself. I kept the introduction fairly simple. I wanted students to know some things about me personally and understand why I would be in their classroom during the coming weeks. I presented myself as a graduate student from the University of North Carolina (UNC) who was working on a research project with the Crow Canyon Archaeological Center.

With North Carolina and Colorado being 2,000 miles apart, I assumed they might have some difficulty figuring out a context for me, so I provided them with two bits of information that I thought seemed relevant to their world. I gave them my account of how Hurricane Fran had ripped through the heart of Carolina a couple of weeks earlier and I talked about UNC "Tarheel" basketball. I found the first topic to be an enormously successful way to engage the students in conversation and the second to be a complete flop. To my dismay, basketball seemed to be of minor importance to these youngsters; thus, the Tarheels carried little meaning for them. In Chapel Hill, North Carolina, basketball is almost a religion; I made the mistake of assuming that this mania also stretched across the nation. Natural disasters, however, are exciting for most kids, and these students had seen some thrilling news coverage of Fran, so being able to give them a first-hand account afforded me a special status. Some of the discussion that ensued, as one might expect, ventured into stories of other powerful storms. As my primary goal was to get the kids talking, I felt I had achieved success.

A second goal for my initial visit was to have students actually understand my research objective; they needed to grasp what I was interested in and what we would be doing together if they were to act as co-researchers. I presented my work by first asking the groups what research is. This proved to be the perfect starting place because I found that the majority had a far better understanding of the research process than I would have imagined. They explained to me that research is looking for answers to questions and that we can use a variety of resources for information including books, newspapers, encyclopedias, computers, the Internet, and people. I told them my question was, "How do kids think about, or picture, the past?" I explained that this question was important to me because I didn't like history when I was in school and had read that a lot of other people felt the same way. I told them I wanted to understand how kids learn about the past so I could develop better ways to teach history. I also told them I couldn't find this information in a book and that they were the experts who could help answer my question.

When a question is posed, we become more conscious of our own thinking in relation to the given topic. The question itself becomes a kind of organizer for thought and we become more alert to information that will contribute to an answer. In explaining my question to the students, I was hoping to cause them to become more reflective regarding their ideas of the past and more ready to share those thoughts freely with me.

Shortly after this first meeting with students, I attended a spaghetti dinner at Dixon Elementary that was their fundraiser for the Crow Canyon field experience. I was curious to know how students would react to me, how they would identify me outside the one place they knew me, which was their classrooms. Their responses were mixed and interesting. Some of them looked at me but didn't seem to know what action to take from there and just moved on. Some engaged in casual conversation and others introduced me to family members. The introductions were amusing and somewhat revealing, indicating that, although the students had friendly feelings toward me, they had difficulty explaining my role to others. In some cases, they associated me with Crow Canyon, sometimes they lumped me into the easily communicated classification of student-teacher but my personal favorite was the little girl who introduced me to her family as "that girl from North Carolina." I couldn't remember the last time anyone called me a girl (as opposed to lady, teacher, etc.), so I was delighted to discover that I still qualified.

The Curriculum

Teaching the Pueblo Past: Classroom Approaches

The methods and materials used for teaching about Pueblo history and culture varied greatly across the project classrooms. I found this surprising because autonomy in program development is not the norm in public schools, particularly in the current climate of educational standards and accountability. I was initially inclined to attribute this independence to the fact that most of the teachers had many years of classroom experience. I knew this assumption was incorrect when I saw that the teachers at South Elementary were as active in fashioning their own curriculum as were the three more experienced teachers at Dixon. I concluded that autonomy was in some way being encouraged or nurtured in the Waterville school system.

I was interested in knowing how the five teachers participating in the project approached curriculum development and if there were some common threads or criteria that held together the diverse instructional approaches that I observed in their classrooms. I found that, regarding the teaching of Colorado history, all of them were relying to some extent on Waterville's *Curriculum Standards for Elementary History*, which were developed locally but based on curriculum standards for the state of Colorado. The standards were posted on the walls of some of the classrooms at Dixon and were part of every teacher's curriculum notebook at South. How closely they were consulting these guidelines in developing units of study is difficult to say, but it appeared that the teachers with the most classroom experience were the least likely to refer to the curriculum standards. One of the Dixon teachers explained that if she were to use curriculum standards, she would be much more likely to use those developed locally than those written at the state or national level. At the time the study was conducted, Waterville's *Curriculum Standards for Elementary History* consisted of six basic objectives:

1. Students will understand the chronological organization of history and know how to group people and events into major eras to identify and explain historical relationships.
2. Students will know how to use various processes and resources of historical inquiry.
3. Students will understand that societies are diverse and have changed over time.
4. Students will understand how science, technology, and economic activity have developed, changed, and affected societies throughout history.
5. Students will understand political institutions and theories that have developed and changed over time.
6. Students will know that religious and philosophical ideas have been powerful forces throughout history.

Four levels of proficiency were identified for these standards: In Progress, Basic, Proficient, and Advanced. In most cases, fourth-grade students were not expected to move beyond the Basic level.

Four of the five teachers participating in the project centered their introduction to Pueblo history around either a core piece of literature or a set of lessons designed by someone else. In these four classrooms, the literature and activities were used prior to the Crow Canyon trip.

The three Dixon teachers expressed an aversion to the use of textbooks for teaching history at the elementary school level. Caroline, who taught at South, was the only teacher among the five who chose to use a textbook. She included readings from a text entitled *Colorado Grassroots* (Schmidt 1989). The text is organized in a roughly chronological fashion, with pairs of short informative pieces and narrative vignettes for each of the fifteen chapters. Caroline also involved her students in learning about the Pueblo past in a number of other ways, including a presentation by the father of one of her students who had written a book for children on southwestern archaeology. Her primary resource for the Pueblo unit was a set of pre-trip lessons provided by the Crow Canyon Archaeological Center. These activities focused on critical thinking skills, particularly inference and on ancestral Pueblo culture.

Betty introduced archaeology to her class through activities from a curriculum that was developed by the Bureau of Land Management (BLM) and published in a teacher's guide called *Intrigue of the Past* (Smith, Moe, Letts, and Paterson 1993). Susan focused primarily on activities from a simulation called *Mahopa*, a product of *Interact*, an educational materials publisher. *Mahopa* doesn't focus on archaeology or critical-thinking skills, but on social organization and the interaction between people and their natural environment. Jean chose to introduce her students to ancestral Pueblo life through literature. She read portions of *The Village of Blue Stone* (Trimble 1990) to her class daily and, as they listened, students were instructed to write down evidence of how the ancestral Pueblo people met their needs across four different seasons.

Of the five teachers participating in this project, Michael was the only one who began the ancestral Pueblo study with the trip to Crow Canyon. He chose this direction for a couple of reasons, primarily because he was unfamiliar with the Crow Canyon program but also because he saw it as a way to launch the unit. Michael felt he could plan the rest of the unit based on the particular areas of interest students developed at Crow Canyon. He also pointed out that this approach would introduce a greater degree of instructional diversity to the research project.

The Crow Canyon Program

The students who participated in this research project were involved in a two-day program at the Crow Canyon Archaeological Center. The three classes from Dixon were divided into two groups for the field experience. Jean Logan's class was split into two groups, with half of them joining Harris's class for the field experience and the other half joining Cole's group. Jean came to Crow Canyon with each of these groups. Table 4.1 shows the schedule for these trips.

The Crow Canyon program varied little for each of the school groups, although a different educator from the Center taught each class. From my observations, I believe each of the groups had similar instructional experiences, with one exception. A young Crow Canyon intern, Steven, led some of the classes during the week of October 28. Steven had less teaching experience than the other instructors did and, while very knowledgeable regarding program content, he was weak in some of the required instructional skills. This was particularly apparent in the way he questioned students and monitored participation. Steven was consistently drawn to the most verbal children in the group, often ignoring quieter students who sat with their hands in the air, waiting to be called on. The quieter

Table 4.1.   Schedule for Field Trip to Crow Canyon Archaeological Center

Classes	Monday	Tuesday	Wednesday	Thursday	Friday
Harris/Logan		Day 1, Oct. 22	Day 2, Oct. 23		
Cole/Logan				Day 1, Oct. 24	Day 2, Oct. 25
Ortiz	Day 1, Oct. 28	Day 2, Oct. 29			
Norton			Day 1, Oct. 30	Day 2, Oct. 31	

students in this group tended to be girls and I worried that Steven's failure to acknowledge them would silence them in future activities. My impression was, however, that they did just the opposite. During the closing discussion of the simulated excavation, the female students *made* the intern notice them; they were quite vocal in the follow-up discussion and often made comments without raising their hands or waiting for Steven to call on them. I wondered if there was something about the lesson itself that encouraged the girls to be more assertive. It is a question that moves outside the parameters of this research project, but this observation suggests to me that the girls found the activity so intellectually engaging that their enthusiasm for it outweighed their learned quiet behavior. It also suggests that Steven inadvertently taught them that the only way to be noticed was to break traditional classroom rules of order. At any rate, Steven's novice teaching skills seemed to be less important to student learning than the activity itself.

Matt Lewis, a Crow Canyon educator for more than eight years, led instruction for the groups from Dixon and Kelly Smith, who had taught at the Center for three years, led the programs for South. Lewis is a highly skilled teacher and had taught in the Waterville school district prior to his employment at Crow Canyon. Coincidentally, Lewis taught both of Betty Harris's children when they were in elementary school. Smith holds a degree in anthropology rather than education but had developed into an insightful and energetic teacher during her years at Crow Canyon. She had a natural rapport with children and was well liked by students who visited the Center. The Crow Canyon instructional components for each of the groups is shown in table 4.2.

As the table shows, the primary difference in programs for each of the groups was the lack of a site tour for the two groups from South elementary. The fieldwork at Crow Canyon had closed down by the last week in October, so the students did not have access to a working archaeological site. This experience was replaced with the Ecohike for Ortiz's class and with the visit to the Anasazi Heritage Center

Table 4.2.   Instructional Components of the Crow Canyon Archaeological Program

Classes	Day 1—A.M.	Day 1—P.M.	Day 2—A.M.	Day 2—P.M.
Harris/Logan	Windows into the Past	Site Tour— Yellow Jacket	Simulated Excavation	Ancient Lifestyles
Cole/Logan	Windows into the Past	Site Tour— Yellow Jacket	Simulated Excavation	Ancient Lifestyles
Ortiz	Ancient Lifestyles	Windows into the Past	Simulated Excavation	Ecohike
Norton	Lifestyles	Windows into the Past	Simulated Excavation	Anasazi Heritage Center

for Norton's. Norton and Otiz made these choices for their students. Each of the Crow Canyon instructional components is described in the following summary.

Windows into the Past

Students worked in cooperative groups to explore five time periods in Pueblo history (Archaic, Basketmaker, Early Farmers, Pueblo Farmers, and Modern Pueblo) through an examination of artifacts, replicas, illustrations, and plant samples. At the conclusion of the inquiry portion of the lesson, students were asked to chronologically order the sets of materials they had been working with. The lesson took about three hours to complete; it established the Pueblo time line that students would be working with for the remainder of the trip. Observation and inference were highlighted and students learned how archaeologists use evidence to construct interpretations of past human activities.

Ancient Lifestyles

This session was taught in, and around, a replicated Basketmaker pithouse. Inside the pithouse, students were encouraged to make observations using all of their senses. They discussed pithouse construction and what life would be like in a pithouse. They also experimented with fire starting using a bow and spindle stick. In the area around the pithouse, students ground corn using a mano and metate, played some traditional Native American games, and experimented with spear throwing using an atlatl.

Site Tour

Students spent between two and three hours touring Yellow Jacket Pueblo. Crow Canyon archaeologists were working on the site at the time of the visit. They discussed architecture with the students and addressed questions. Instructors from Crow Canyon directed students' attention to the natural landscape and guided them in thinking about why people would have chosen to locate their homes in that particular place. They also helped students identify artifacts and conveyed to them the importance of leaving artifacts in the exact location in which they are found.

Ecohike

In this activity, students were shown some of the common plants of the area and taught to identify them. In the second part of the lesson, they divided into groups to complete a scavenger hunt focusing on traditional uses of the plants by native peoples of the Southwest.

Simulated Excavation

This three- to four-hour activity involved students in excavating archaeological sites that were simulated in a sandbox. There were three separate sandboxes, two that corresponded to earlier Pueblo sites and one that represented the late Pueblo period. Students were led through the archaeological research process; they were asked to formulate research questions and then learned excavation methods. Throughout the session, they were required to record notes on an excavation form. When their units were completely excavated, they mapped the location of the objects that were found on the floor. As a group, they made inferences about the site, based on the material evidence, and attempted to answer their research questions.

Anasazi Heritage Center

This museum provides visitors with a video presentation of Pueblo history and exhibits some of the artifacts from its extensive collection. The center, which is under the direction of the BLM, curates the materials from Crow Canyon excavations as well as from other archaeological research projects in the area. The heritage center has a number of excellent exhibits, such as a simulated stratigraphic profile, interactive computer stations, and displays of ancestral Pueblo artifacts. Escalante Pueblo, a Pueblo II period site, is within a short walk of the heritage center.

Pieces of the Past

5

Making Sense of the Data

ANALYZING QUALITATIVE DATA IS A DAUNTING TASK, for it generally requires organization of very large data sets that contain information that is diverse in both form and content. Where there is little prior research to build on, as in this case study, the scope of data collection is, of necessity, rather expansive. I began this study by posing a very broad question, "How do children construct the past; how do they make meaning of it?" To explore this question in a manageable way, two sets of guiding questions were developed to focus data collection; these addressed two aspects of the research. The first set dealt with the material of student constructions—knowledge and beliefs about Pueblo life in the past—and the second with the use of those elements in constructing meaning.

- Questions regarding students knowledge and beliefs:
  - What do these fourth graders know about the Pueblo past?
    (Information that students would classify as factual.)
  - What beliefs or attitudes do they hold regarding the Pueblo past?
  - Do knowledge and beliefs change as students move through the unit of study?
- Questions regarding the construction of meaning:
  - What is the nature of individual student constructions?
  - Do students construct the past in similar ways? Are there similar themes in their construction?

I did not venture into this project without having some idea of how these questions might be answered. While I expected to see some similarity in the ways children conceptualize the past, I also believed patterns might emerge that were more related to culture, community, and family than to age. And, as is typical in qualitative research, certain issues emerged in the field that led me down new paths I had not anticipated prior to working on the project. In this study, as in most qualitative projects, analysis was an on-going process. What I saw and heard in the field, what participants told me during interviews, or what they let me see through their work were daily guiding forces that helped shape my understanding and direct my attention.

Data Analysis

Analysis of the project data is organized around the central and refining questions posed at the beginning of the research process. In each of these areas, I rely almost entirely on cross-case analysis of the data. The primary exception to this is an analysis of fifteen in-depth interviews. These were assessed in a within-case, as well as in a cross-case, manner. This decision was based on the nature of student responses; I found that to understand how children were making meaning of the past, I had to understand their narratives in the context of each of their personalities. I then took the findings from the within-case analyses and did a cross-case comparison to search for patterns in the way children were constructing their knowledge. I used the same approach in analyzing some of the data obtained through the observations. Although I looked first for information that helped me understand the group, I sometimes found that I could not interpret what the group was about until I had unraveled what was happening with some of the key members. For example, if an individual made comments that seemed a bit off-track, I found that pursuing her or his train of thought often led me to recognize that other children held a similar perspective. In a large sense, these key individuals were more expressive than others in their classroom—they provided a lens through which to view the group.

Another critical aspect of analyzing these data is the use of triangulation, a method for checking the consistency of findings generated by different types of qualitative data (Patton 1990). The value in amassing a large amount of data, and from different sources, is that it provides multiple ways to examine and verify research findings and, thus, helps establish both validity and reliability.

All methods for gathering information proved valuable, but the most useful instruments were the concept maps, the lists of things children said they knew and wanted to know regarding the Pueblo past, the in-depth interviews, and the surveys (see appendix 2 for survey form and interview guide).

Concept maps are a type of graphic organizer that can illustrate the information an individual considers important regarding a particular topic and it also shows the meaningful relationships constructed between these bits of information. Concept maps can help clarify the small number of key ideas for both teachers and students for a specific learning task. A map can also provide a kind of visual road map showing some of the pathways we may take to connect meanings of concepts in propositions. After a learning task has been completed, concept maps provide a schematic summary of what has been learned. [Novak and Gowin 1984]

These maps, like other forms of educational assessment, provide only a partial view of the way an individual thinks about a particular concept. What can be learned through the use of concept maps is, first of all, limited by the fact that they require a good deal of writing. Students who have poor writing skills or who have an aversion to writing, will not show all that they know because it simply seems like too great a task. Younger children may have difficulty with the hierarchical structure that is a fundamental aspect of concept maps. Most fourth graders have probably had experience with this kind of classification, but it is unlikely that all will have mastered it. In this project, the concept map process was facilitated by the fact that the participating teachers regularly used a similar strategy with students as a prewriting activity. Thus, the majority of these students were quick to understand how the maps should be structured.

Children constructed the concept maps at the beginning of the research period and revised them after their field trip to Crow Canyon Archaeological Center, approximately five weeks later. The teachers administered the surveys after the formal research period had ended. Data from one class (Ortiz) were incomplete in that the survey forms were not returned and many of the students were not present for the follow-up session where they were given the opportunity to revise their concept maps. I did, however, have more than eighty maps and surveys to work from and felt that this was a large enough sample to reveal patterns in student thinking and provide redundancy in responses.

The concept maps were rich with information regarding the children's knowledge of the Pueblo past and with the ways in which they were organizing that information. I introduced students to concept maps by helping them construct one that illustrated life in Waterville (see chapter 4). We completed this as a group, with students generating the content while I recorded their thoughts on the whiteboard. As we worked, I talked with them about the components of a concept map and helped them with structure. I explained that the central topic is followed by big ideas, which serve as categories for organizing information, and that information related to these big ideas should follow. After they constructed the basic map, I asked them to look for areas that were connected in some way and we drew in lines to illustrate those connections, then talked about words that could be used to describe the connections. When I felt satisfied that students had grasped the steps in making a concept map, and after we had built a fairly elaborate one for

Waterville life, I assigned them each the task of constructing a map of ancestral Pueblo/Anasazi life. These maps were used in several ways—first, as a guide for selecting the students who would be interviewed; second, to reveal what students knew of the Pueblo past; and third, to track conceptual change.

After all classes completed the concept maps, I looked for patterns across them that might prove useful in structuring the data collection. The maps fell easily into one of three categories: (1) those showing an exceptionally high knowledge level; (2) those showing an average knowledge level (where most of the students were performing); and (3) those showing stereotypical information, misconceptions, and a mix of time periods and cultural groups (these most often contained pan-Indian or caveman images). I then selected fifteen students to interview based on these three categories (table 5.1).

My goal was to select one student from every category out of each of the five classrooms. In reality, I varied somewhat from my original plan for selection of interviewees. It was difficult to connect with some of the students I had originally targeted, due to absences or schedule changes. I felt it was more important to have each of the categories fairly represented than to have the same number of students from each class. Thus, I decided, in a couple of cases, to interview four students from one class and two from another.

Knowledge of Ancestral Pueblo Life

A constructivist perspective assumes that prior knowledge exists before formal instruction takes place and that a child's mind is not a blank slate. Even though I

Table 5.1. Students Selected for In-depth Interviews. Numbers in column 5 correspond to (1) high knowledge level, (2) average knowledge level, and (3) stereotypical images, misconceptions, and/or culture/time mix.

Student	School	Teacher	Gender	Category
Ricky	Dixon	Cole	M	3
Martin	Dixon	Harris	M	3
Brian	Dixon	Logan	M	2
Albert	South	Norton	M	3
Crystal	Dixon	Cole	F	3
Mary	South	Norton	F	2
Brad	South	Norton	M	2
Taylor	Dixon	Harris	F	1
Martha	South	Norton	F	1
Carla	Dixon	Cole	F	1
Kari	South	Ortiz	F	1
Jill	South	Ortiz	F	2
April	Dixon	Harris	F	2
Murphy	Dixon	Logan	F	3
Randy	Dixon	Cole	M	1

approached the research project from this perspective, I was still amazed to learn just how much the students already knew about Pueblo life in the past. Although they were just beginning their unit of study when I had them create the concept maps, most of the students demonstrated a good deal of prior experience with the topic.

Analysis of the maps showed that most of the information recorded at the start of the project was highly concrete in nature. The Pueblo past represented with these maps was an object filled world that was defined by meeting basic human needs. The primary categories that appeared across virtually all of the maps were food, shelter/homes, clothing, and subsistence (recorded by the students as hunting, farming, and gathering). This was true regardless of which school students attended or who their teacher was. Most students branched out from these categories with long lists of examples. Corn, which is considered central to Pueblo life, was included on virtually every map. It was apparent that all students knew that you do not talk about Pueblo life, past or present, without talking about corn. Other kinds of food most often identified were squash, beans, berries, deer, rabbits, and turkeys. Students who took a more descriptive, rather than functional, approach tended to list these same items under the headings of plants or animals. A variety of house types were listed, with the most frequent being cliff dwelling. Kiva and pueblo appeared on a lot of the maps, as did the names of building materials such as stone, mud, sticks, and adobe. I was surprised that a lot of the students included a particular method of pueblo construction called "waddle and daub." Some of them had a little difficulty with the term, and it appeared in various forms, such as "wobble and dob"; the meaning, however, was still clear.

The most common classifications given, other than those related to basic needs, were pottery, tools, and weather. Although it would seem logical to list pottery as an example of a type of container, or even as art, most students seemed to let pottery stand alone. The words most often linked to pottery included designs, black-and-white paint, and clay. Tools were sometimes listed as weapons. Although these are very different in meaning, the associated examples were virtually the same regardless of the term given. Apparently, for some students, knives, arrows, and spears were instruments for doing work and for others they were intended for more aggressive purposes. Weather was important on some of the maps, but mostly in relation to precipitation. Over the last couple of decades, drought has been given as a major explanation for why the Pueblo people left the northern San Juan region by A.D. 1300. In terms of sophistication of thought, weather and climate would rank higher than basic needs. A few of the students made the connection that basic needs are directly affected by environmental conditions. Beyond the shared emphases on basic human needs, the concept maps varied greatly. Some students listed jobs or work, some included people, and several included art as a part of the ancestral Pueblo world. When art was listed, several other links were generally included, such as petroglyphs and paint.

An important aspect of concept maps is that of cross-linked information. A cross-link is where an individual recognizes the relationship between two concepts that originated from separate strands of the main idea and then connects these concepts on the map by drawing a line between them. A large number of cross-links generally indicate a more complex and sophisticated understanding of the topic. The average number of cross-links on the first version of the maps was 2.5, and the range was 0–8. This indicates that the majority of students were structuring what they knew of the Pueblo past in a fairly simple and basic fashion.

Approximately two weeks after the project had started, Norton and Cole had their students generate a list of things they knew about ancestral Pueblo life and a list of questions reflecting the things they wanted to know. While not identical to the content of the concept maps, there was a great deal of similarity. Students said they knew that these ancient people had been hunters and farmers; that they ate corn, beans, and squash; and that their houses were built of stone, mud, and sticks. However, these lists moved slightly away from the object-centered constructions to include some evaluative statements and to comment on the quality of life:

"They were no different than us."

"They always changed over time."

"They worked hard all the time."

"They had short lives."

"They gathered together for spiritual prayers and dances."

These comments, particularly the first three, are significantly different in nature than those the students recorded on their concept maps. The open discussions that generated these lists might have allowed some students to express views more easily than did the concept map format, or it could be that hearing the views of others helped some individuals make connections that led to these conclusions.

An account of what students knew about the Pueblo past when the project started must also include what they did not know or, at least, appeared not to know. Both the concept maps and the lists made by the two classes included a good bit of information that was incorrect. The most common misconceptions were that ancestral Pueblo people lived in hogans and/or teepees, that they had horses and cattle, and that they tended sheep. A less frequent but repeated idea was that mammoth and saber tooth tiger hunting was a part of Pueblo culture in ancient times. These notions reflected a mixing of cultural groups or time periods and in some cases both. A hogan is a traditional Navajo dwelling. According to most southwestern archaeologists, the Navajos moved into the Four Corners long after the last Pueblo people left. Ute people living in the area used teepees but, like the Navajo, also appear to have not entered the Four Corners until after the Pueblo people left the region.

In addition to what I am calling misconceptions, were a number of stereotypical images of Native people that reflected the "savage Indian" myth. I was surprised to see words like tomahawk and war paint on some of the concept maps. Occasionally, students wrote about the physical appearance of the ancestral Pueblo people. Among some of the more generally accepted ideas, like having black hair, being short in stature, and having poor teeth, were descriptors like "naked," "hair covered," and "black." Classroom observations also revealed some classic stereotypes of American Indians. When Susan Cole's class first divided into different tribes for their *Mahopa* simulation, some of the students began to speak in what sounded like an electronic or robotic voice. It was somewhat like the choppy Indian-English of the old Hollywood westerns, but the content was closer to that of a *Star Wars* movie. Perhaps it was actually a blend of *The Lone Ranger*, *Star Wars*, and *Dances with Wolves*. What was obvious was that, for some of these students, being Indian required a way of speaking that was different than their ordinary way of conversing.

I felt it was important to distinguish between what children meant by some of these expressions and what I was assuming they meant. The information students gave that related to basic needs seemed fairly straightforward, but I was less convinced that I understood why they said the ancestral Pueblo people were naked and covered with hair. I also wanted to know if students were as confused about the different cultures and time periods as some of their work indicated. These were the primary reasons I chose to have a third of the interview group consist of students whose work had reflected such misconceptions and stereotypes.

The interviews were quite revealing and helped clarify what students knew about the Pueblo past at the start of this project. During one part of the interview process, I showed each student her or his concept map and asked her or him to tell me about it. Most of them gave a very literal explanation, telling me little more than I had understood on my own. However, when I asked specific questions such as, "You have horses on your map; when did the ancestral Pueblo people get horses?" Students would give the correct response—that horses came with the Spaniards or Europeans and that Pueblo people had them later in time. Most of the students who included hogans said they were not really sure if Pueblo people used them. Those who included teepees gave several different explanations:

"Well, it's just kind of an Indian thing, so I put it in."

"If they traveled around, like to go on hunting trips, they must have had some kind of tent."

"No, the plains people used teepees, I don't know why I put it there."

The first student's explanation for the teepee misconception might be described as a stereotype but it also poses the question: when should an object be considered an icon rather than a stereotype, or are the two the same? Most students who included teepees knew that they weren't used by Pueblo people but felt that it was OK to include them. It seems possible that for some of these students, a teepee is symbolic of Indians, in the same way that a trowel has become an icon for archaeology. Excavation represents only a small percentage of the time spent in archaeological research, but the trowel has become the symbol of the profession and is likely to remain so for years to come. The line that separates icon from stereotype is a fuzzy one; both are oversimplified generalizations. Sometimes icons are also stereotypes, for example, the mountain people of southern Appalachia have often been reduced to the image of a barefoot, toothless man dressed in patched overalls and carrying a moonshine jug. This is a harmful icon or stereotype because it belittles mountain people and conveys a negative image of Appalachian people to the rest of the world. Teepees may be an oversimplified symbol of Indian things for some of the students, but it's not necessarily a harmful symbol.

The student who reasoned that the ancestral Pueblo people must have had something like a teepee or tent that they could use when they went hunting was assuming that people in the past would solve problems in the same way as those in the present. His assumption regarding the need for a tent when you go hunting was stronger than the information he had encountered regarding the lack of use of teepees by ancestral Pueblo people. The difficulty of removing the lens of the present when we interpret the past may be at the heart of many misconceptions regarding history (Wineburg 2001).

Sometimes images are so ingrained that they are taken for granted. Such illusions are difficult to undo because they are accepted as being the way things are. The explanation given by the third student may fall into this category. She knew that the ancestral Pueblo people did not use teepees, yet she included them and could not explain why.

Some concepts were more confusing for students than others, particularly the aspects of Pueblo culture that have changed over time. In modern times, sheep herding and weaving with wool have been important to the lives of all Native peoples in the Four Corners. However, the sheep that are grown for wool are not indigenous to North America; white settlers and the U.S. government were responsible for introducing domesticated sheep in the Southwest. When I quizzed students about this, they generally seemed to think their information was accurate. Because the idea was so prominent, I asked them where they learned about Pueblo people raising sheep. All students said they had learned it from a video. I knew about the video they spoke of; it is designed to show the continuity and change in Pueblo life. It focuses on the deep history of Pueblo culture, but much of the footage is of active, contemporary Pueblo people. Even though the narration in the video differentiates between past and present, the images of the people seemed to blend into one time period for the children.

Students who included mammoths and saber-toothed tigers in their construction of the Pueblo past explained their inclusion in one of two ways:

"Well, they didn't do that when they were living in Pueblos; that was earlier."

"I saw it in a book. They followed them (megafauna) across the land bridge."

One of the students, Ricky, who had described ancient Pueblo people as being naked and covered with hair explained his perception in a manner that was quite surprising. I assumed his impression came from cartoon images of cavemen. When I asked Ricky where he got the idea that ancestral Pueblo people had hair all over, he responded: "Well, because of the books I read. I get these different books, I used to get *Zoo Books* and one of them was telling about apes and how scientists think people were like apes and then they kind of changed. I don't think they were really like people until they changed again." When I asked Ricky if he had been reading about evolution, his face brightened and he replied enthusiastically that he had.

It seems that Ricky and these other students did not fully understand the concept of culture and, as a result, had difficulty identifying cultural differences. They made the connection that the ancestral Pueblo people must have descended from those who crossed the Bering Land Bridge, just as other groups of Native Americans had. Ricky was trying to imagine ancient people as far back as modern science has been able to grasp, and others were making the connection between the Pueblo people of today and those who occupied the Four Corners over 700 years ago.

The materials the students had encountered, such as the books and videos, made historical connections between peoples, but the students were either missing, or had not gotten, information that helped them understand the meaning of culture. They were correct about the human connections they were making across time, but they weren't placing them within the paradigm of culture. The same might be said for some of the students who placed hogans and teepees within Pueblo culture. It seems that they lacked a sufficient understanding of culture so, when I asked questions about Pueblo culture, they did not have adequate knowledge to appropriately address the questions. In a sense, we were talking past each other.

There was an interesting contrast between what children reported knowing and their questions expressing what they wanted to know. The concept maps and lists of knowledge reflected a largely concrete understanding of ancestral Pueblo life. Students also talked of beliefs and opinions they held regarding the Pueblo past, but when asked for knowledge, they described an object-centered past. Their questions regarding what they would like to learn about the Pueblo past at Crow Canyon were of a different nature, focusing far more on abstract concepts. Table 5.2 illustrates this contrast between what the children said they knew and what they were curious to learn more about.

The table is a compilation of student questions and comments. Redundant comments have been omitted. The first column, "What I Know" is filled with bits of information that tells about the material goods of the ancestral Pueblo people, the work they did, and where they lived. The questions in the second column seem to indicate that students are not interested in learning more about the basic facts of everyday Pueblo life. Their questions may be broken down into two categories: research questions and self, or child-centered, questions. Questions regarding length of antiquity, occupation, migration, population, and conflict are compara-

Table 5.2.   Knowledge and Questions Regarding the Pueblo Past

What I Know	What I Want to Learn
They lived in and on the cliffs.	Why did they choose to live in caves?
They had to plant their food and they had to hunt for food.	What did they do for a living?
They made their houses out of rocks and mud.	How did they get ideas for their houses?
	How old are the ruins at Crow Canyon?
	How long did they live there?
They were scattered all over the place.	What language did they speak?
They had to work hard.	What/how did they learn? Was there a school?
They are gone.	Why are they gone?
They grew and ate corn, squash, and beans.	What did they do for fun?
They "weaved" rugs and made baskets.	What did they do to get ready for winter?
They had big meeting areas.	How many (people) were there?
They lived in the Southwest.	Where did the Anasazi come from?
	Did they move more than once?
	Where did they go?
They used atlatls and spears to hunt animals.	How did they learn to hunt?
They had shamans.	How many enemies did they have? Who were their most feared enemies?
They made petroglyphs and pottery.	
They made good designs.	

ble to those of professional archaeologists who are interested in understanding the social world of the ancestral Pueblo people. I can't say for sure why the students were interested in these issues, but I suspect that their reasons are not very dissimilar from those of adults who pose the same questions. Deserted communities seem to haunt us. We look at their vacant shells and get the feeling that something went wrong, and we want to understand what that might have been.

A number of other questions posed by students seemed to focus on issues that are important to a child's world. Many were about learning and these might be viewed in several ways. The work of schoolchildren is to learn; much of a child's world revolves around schooling and issues of learning. I believe that most of the children in the study who asked this question already thought they had an answer. When the topic came up in group discussions, there were always students with a ready answer, one that the rest of the group seemed to support. Students generally said that you would learn from someone else, by watching and practicing. The same scenario was also given in a number of the stories students told in the interviews. If students believed they already had the answer, why did they so often pose the question? Perhaps they were saying that learning is a huge part of living and they think it is important to consider how learning would have happened in the Pueblo past. They would not have labeled their beliefs about learning as knowledge because they recognize that no evidence exists to support this point of view. It's also possible that they were pointing to the fact that school is not necessary for learning; in some cases, learning and schools may even be oppositional issues for children. A third explanation would be that students are using learning as a bridge between their world and the Pueblo past; it might be a point of intersection that serves to make the past more real. In the same vein, students may wonder about fun or play because it is also central to their world. If we tend to view the past through our own personality and identity, then it would follow that elementary school age children might use learning, work, and play to make connections with the past.

Regardless of why children asked what they did, the clear message was that they wanted to understand more advanced and complex things about the Pueblo past than how people met their basic needs. When materials are developed for history instruction in the elementary grades, the authors often operate under the assumption that children of this age can't process abstract concepts. I would argue that children who are asking questions about migration and language are ready to learn about more than corn, beans, and squash.

Culture is an abstract concept; while it does encompass the material world and basic patterns of subsistence, it is far more than that. If we profess to be teaching children about culture, then we also need to introduce them to the social aspects of culture as well as the concrete manifestations. Where culture is reduced to a set of objects, subsistence patterns, and architectural style, it is not surprising that students become confused by the subtle differences they are shown between different groups of Native Americans. At the heart of understanding culture is being able to answer the question, "What makes a Navajo, Navajo or what makes a Hopi, Hopi?" If we do not focus on issues that can help students answer those questions, it may be difficult for them to see Navajo or Hopi as anything but Indian.

Anthropologists have sometimes referred to culture as the human toolkit for survival. A shared understanding of symbolic systems allows us to organize and make sense of our world in communicable ways. Culture colors our perception of the world and establishes our sense of normalcy, order, and logic. Archaeologist David Hurst Thomas is credited with the often-quoted phrase, "It's not what you find, it's what you find out." To present a culture's past as the objects they made and used would be the antithesis of this statement. Just as isolated artifacts removed from their original context contribute little to an archaeological understanding of the people who made them, history or heritage instruction that doesn't move beyond a discussion of objects isn't likely to help students develop a more sophisticated understanding of past cultures.

Beliefs about Ancestral Pueblo Life

Beyond what children knew of the past, this study looked at what they believed about the Pueblo past. A common perception that many people have regarding the past is that life was more difficult then than it is now. The majority of students interviewed for this project (twelve of the fifteen) agreed with this perspective.

> I think life was a little harder back then because they didn't have calculators or computers to figure problems out. I'm not sure, but I don't think they had schools, and I know they couldn't just drive to the grocery store because they didn't have a car and there was no grocery store. [Brad]

> Maybe it was a little bit harder then, like when you were getting water—you could get sick because the water was from streams. Or you could get food poisoning from stuff you pick off the ground. [Martin]

> It was probably a little harder then because you had to carry big things, like if they lived on top of the mesa, they had to walk back up and they had to carry baskets on their back with water in them. [Martha]

> It would be harder back then because you would have to walk everywhere on foot and it would take a long time. And you would have to build everything by hand. [Brian]

Although these students said that life for the ancestral Pueblo people was harder than it is in modern times, some of the same children also said they thought it would have been more fun:

I think it would be funner. You'd have to work more but then you could have more play time I think. Like here you go to school and then you go home and do your homework and sometimes you have time to play, and then. . . . I think they might have worked in the morning and played in the afternoon. [Ricky]

The three students who did not think life was harder in ancestral Pueblo times said they thought it was just different than now:

Life was just different for them, they actually had the same kind of life only they had to do it in different ways. . . . They made clothes, we make clothes, they had jobs, we have jobs, they cooked and had animals, they also had plants growing in a garden. [Murphy]

I think it was a lot different than it is now. . . . I don't really like all of the pollution and stuff like a lot of the technology—I do like computers, but I think it would be fun to live in the Anasazi age and the Victorian age. . . . I live on Third Avenue and in the morning I wake up really early because of all the loud cars and stuff like that. [Mary]

It was kind of the same as now because we don't need all the things we have, we could live without all of them. . . . We still build our houses like they did and we still gather and hunt and stuff like that. And of course we still grow stuff. [Taylor]

All three students agreed that the past was just different than now, but each had a unique perspective on the nature of that difference. Murphy's view tends to mirror that of the concept maps, it is a comparison that is grounded in basic human needs. To her, the differences are more an issue of style or form. Taylor's view is similar but she seems to be seeing a kind of excess in the modern world that Murphy does not mention. Mary is presenting a perspective that is often associated with older adults; she seems to be yearning for a cleaner, quieter world.

I think it is important to recognize that although all of these students were able to imagine how the past would have been different or harder, this shouldn't be confused with the way they value the past. Merriman (1991) and others have interpreted these expressions of a harder past as being analogous to a past that is worse than the present. I'm not convinced that these are the same. Ricky's words expressed a point of view I believe others share—that the past was harder but, in his words, "funner."

It has been suggested that what children know and believe about the past may, to some extent, be a function of what they are developmentally capable of. The teachers from Dixon all expressed the belief that most fourth graders are not really ready to understand deep time. Are there developmental limitations and constraints on the ways that children construct knowledge about the past? Montangero suggested that children the age of those in this study have not yet moved into diachronic thinking, a skill that would seem essential to an understanding of time. He said they are interested in change but have difficulty predicting successive stages and seeing causal relationships. In a diachronic perspective, according to Montangero (1996), the nature of things is to transform. I was interested in exploring his theory that children between the ages of seven and nine tend to view the past as a set of static snapshots and don't transition into seeing the past as more of a moving picture until around nine or ten; most of the children in this study were nine and a few had already turned ten. One of the ways I attempted to get at these issues of change and thinking across time that were raised by Montangero was to ask students if the ancestral Pueblo people always lived the same way across time, or if they changed. The unanimous response was that they changed:

> I think they changed. Scientists think they came down from Alaska, well that's what I've heard at least, and then by the time they had traveled to all the different lands, like snow, to farmlands, to Rocky Mountains, they would have had to change . . . when they moved down, they probably ate wooly mammoth, then when they got here they probably ate buffalo, then when they got all the way down here, they probably ate turkeys and maybe buffalo and deer. [Ricky]

> I think things changed because, like nowadays, people invent new things. Like the kiva, they didn't have it earlier and they had to invent it. [Kari]

> I think things changed, like when they—I don't know if this is true—but I think they got horses later. And they invented new things, like wooden tools or tools of bone and things like that. [Brian]

> They changed. First they were gatherers, then about, say, 300 years later they started hunting, in about another 300 years they probably invented or saw somebody with the bow, they probably met another Indian tribe and saw how they made arrows. [Martin]

> They would have changed . . . like now we use guns, and they used to use bow and arrow. [Albert]

> Well they probably changed because, if they stayed the same, all their food would be gone and they couldn't find anything to eat. So they had to try different kinds of things to eat. [Crystal]

> I think things changed, like they might have cut down all the trees for firewood and then they might have had to move because all the animals would die. [Brad]

> Things changed, because I learned last year that there was the basket weaving period and the hunting period and the growing period. [Carla]

Several observations may be made regarding these responses. To begin, these students were saying that things *had* to change. While they may each be stating it a bit differently, their constructions are not the static snapshots Montangero speaks of. The children were, instead, linking events together in a causal way. Some of these are more concrete links and some are abstract. Carla was, in effect, saying, "I know they changed because this is what I learned from an authoritative source." Brian, Ricky, and Martin were reaching their conclusions similarly but were also constructing their own knowledge based on information from different sources. Kari and Albert were using analogous thinking. They recognized that life in modern human society changes, and they reasoned that it must have been the same for people hundreds of years ago. Brad and Crystal seemed to be exhibiting the kind of true diachronic thinking Montangero says is not common at this age. They were able to conceptualize what the consequences to the environment would be if life did not change.

In one way or another, all the students seem to be saying that the nature of things is to transform. Some of them referred to authority to support their beliefs rather than construct their own understanding but their conviction, nevertheless, was that life is, and has been, a moving picture. An explanation within Montangero's paradigm would be that these students were moving through the transition to diachronic thinking. While this is possible, it does not seem likely that all of the students who, according to his theory, are on the cusp of this developmental transition would have already moved through it. I am not suggesting that this evidence is sufficient to refute Montangero's ideas but I do believe it raises challenging questions and suggests the need to consider alternative paradigms for explaining how the students in this study were understanding change.

Lev Vygotsky has asserted that instruction can lead development and that development cannot be separated from its social context (as quotes in van der Veer and Valsiner 1994). I find this theoretical approach to be compelling and believe it has great explanatory power regarding the ability of the students in this study to think in evolutive ways. The majority of students in this study had a remarkably strong background in Pueblo history. Their second- and third-grade classes had taken field trips to archaeological sites that the children still spoke of and they talked about things they had learned from former teachers, from books, and from museums.

The geographic fabric of the Four Corners area is heavily imprinted with the Pueblo past. If an understanding of time is still a developmental challenge for children of this age, then it might be said that the learning experiences they have been immersed in have led their development. However, those children who based their conclusions regarding change on logic rather than knowledge of the Pueblo time line seem to be doing something different. The knowledge these students applied is knowledge of the social world and of the environment. Most fourth graders have had some experience with environmental education, so, for some of them, learning about the environment may have led their thinking about change and about the past. Those students who reasoned that past cultures changed because present cultures change are applying what they have learned from life experience. The sophistication of thought exhibited by many of these students in their rationales for change are, in my mind, sufficient cause to question any notions of developmental limitations on their ability to think in evolutive ways.

Conceptual Change

Although the process of concept formation and change was observed and recorded throughout the study period, student perceptions were not documented again in any comprehensive way until after the field trip to Crow Canyon. During the first week of November, and the sixth week of the study period, students in each of the five classes were given the opportunity to revise their concept maps. I reviewed the concept map structure and invited them to evaluate what they had written six weeks earlier. Then they were each given a colored pencil and asked to revise their maps, as needed, to reflect what they currently thought. They had drawn the original maps with plain gray lead pencils, so I assumed that the color would allow me to view changes in their knowledge and the way that it was structured. This was true in most cases. There were, however, a couple of students who became carried away with the colored pencils and retraced original lines and words as well, preventing me from making the comparison. Excluding these, I was still left with eighty concept maps to draw information from. Students were also given the option of making no changes if they were happy with the map as it had originally been drawn. A large majority of the students chose to make changes in their maps (70 percent), but there was an interesting difference in results when broken into individual classes, as shown in table 5.3. Because a number of the students from Michael Ortiz's class didn't have an opportunity to revise their maps, figures for his class are not shown.

Table 5.3.   Percentage of Students Who Chose to Modify Their Concept Maps

Teacher/Class	Percent
Norton	85%
Logan	60%
Harris	68%
Cole	66%
All students	70%

The numbers from Dixon elementary (Logan, Harris, and Cole) are all within a few percentage points of one another and all of them, especially Logan's, are lower than the one class that was represented from South elementary. Because data from Ortiz's class were not available, any comparisons made here are, out of necessity, between schools rather than within schools. A number of factors could account for whether or not a student would choose to modify her or his concept map, some of which have nothing to do with conceptual change. Some students may have simply made the choice to not do more work, and those classes with lower results might have more students who are likely to take this route.

Teacher expectations might also influence a student's choice, as might the time of day when the task was assigned. However, these expectations do not seem adequate to explain the differences between Norton's class and the other three. It does not seem reasonable that all three of the classes at Dixon would have had more students with task avoidance than Norton did in her class, and my observations in the classrooms would support this conclusion. The time of day in which students worked on the task also seems an insufficient explanation, as Norton's class completed the activity later in the school day than did any of the others. Students in this class modified their concept maps during the last hour of the school day, which is often the least productive time. Teacher expectations are a powerful influence on student work and Caroline Norton is a teacher with high expectations, but the teachers at Dixon also expected their students to be productive.

There is, however, one explanation for the discrepancy between the number of revised concept maps between the two schools that I believe is worth considering. There was an important difference between Dixon and South schools in the way the Crow Canyon field trip was structured. The three classes from Dixon were divided into two groups that went to Crow Canyon on separate field trips. Dividing the groups meant that one of the classes, Logan's, had to be split; half of the students took the trip with Cole's class and the other half with Harris's class. Jean Logan accompanied each of her groups to Crow Canyon, but I believe the regrouping of students from Dixon for the field trip may have created a different dynamic that might have had an impact on student achievement. Social interaction is always a significant part of the learning equation and field trips are highly social experiences for children, particularly overnight trips.

Teachers often see these enhanced social experiences as ideal for building cooperation and a sense of community among their students. This sort of bonding works best when the group is unified and cohesive. In blending the students from the three Dixon classes, the potential for building individual classroom or group identity may have been diminished. When students have an opportunity to interact with friends they do not usually see in the normal school routine, social issues may sometimes take priority over even the most stimulating learning experiences. In addition to the social considerations, are the educational factors. Caroline Norton was able to help her students relate what they were learning at Crow Canyon to things they had learned in the classroom. When groups are mixed, and when the pretrip instruction is different for each group, as it was with the Dixon students, it is more difficult for teachers to help their students make these connections.

The most notable aspect of the revised concept maps was not so much the quantity of changes as it was the quality of them. Elaboration and complexity characterize the nature of the changes made to many of the concept maps. Students embellished on the basic categories from the original maps (food, shelter, clothing and subsistence) by adding many new examples. These additions consisted almost entirely of artifacts or ideas students had encountered at Crow Canyon. Houses were no longer just cliff dwellings or a list of building materials; the revised maps showed that homes included rooms, kivas, towers, pit structures, and middens. The maps became more sophisticated in both the number of cross-links students were making and in the types of new categories they were including.

Some of the new categories grew out of classifications used in the *Windows into the Past* activity that students participated in at Crow Canyon. However, the most impressive changes were those that tended to reach beyond the concrete world of objects to include more information about things like climate, weather, work, and geography. On the early maps, very little was said about spiritual or esthetic aspects of culture, but on the revised maps, art, games, stories, dances, religion, and ceremony appeared regularly. While none of the first maps included references to time, some of the revisions included notes about things that would have occurred earlier or later. One of the students incorporated time into her revisions by adding a category called "Time Periods," with three links identified as "Basketmaker," Early Farmers," and "Pueblo Farmers." Another student illustrated an amazing leap in his understanding of tradition and culture, as shown in figure 5.1.

Another significant change in the maps had to do with both the number and quality of new cross-links the students were making. A great many students who made minimal additions to their maps in the way of adding new terms, made a significant number of additional cross-links to indicate relationships between things that they had not previously recognized. Some of these cross-links indicated that students were engaged in critical thinking. For example, one student made a connection between "Pot sherds," and "Lots of People." The words written on the link indicated that the student had inferred from the numerous sherds at Yellow Jacket Pueblo that a great number of people must have lived there.

Although many additions were made to most of the maps, there were very few deletions. Certain aspects of the maps that I expected to see change remained consistently the same. The mix of cultures and time periods were generally not changed, although a few students wrote the comments "earlier" and "later" beside

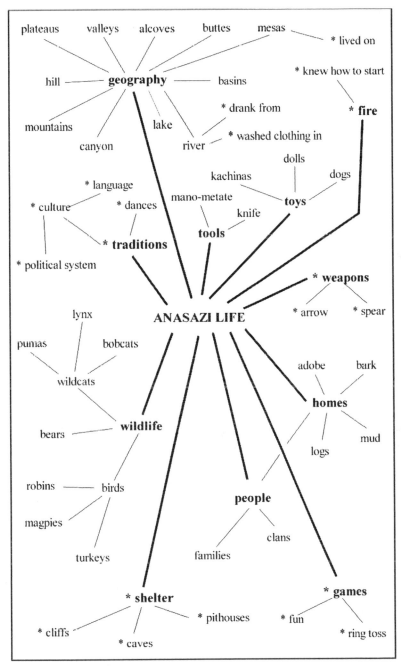

Figure 5.1. Concept Map Showing a Student's Construction of Ancestral Pueblo Life (Bold print indicates primary categories, [*] indicates revisions)

Table 5.4.   Misconceptions According to Gender

Level of Understanding	Girls	Boys
Misconceptions	19 (53%)	22 (48%)
No Misconceptions	17 (47%)	24 (52%)
Total	36	46

certain items on their maps. And where "culture" or "time period" was given as a discrete category, there were no mixes of time and culture. In essence, when students chose culture or time period as a classification system—as a part of the map's structure—the culture/time mix disappeared.

Follow-up surveys were another way I looked at student constructions following the unit of study. Four of the teachers in the project—Norton, Logan, Harris, and Cole—gave their students the follow-up survey within a few weeks after the field trip to Crow Canyon (see appendix 3 for the follow-up survey). Several of the items on the survey were designed to get at issues that emerged through other data. Item 4 asked students to select from a list, those things that would have been a part of ancestral Pueblo life. Included in the choices were the most common misconceptions students made in the concept maps: horses, teepees, mammoths, and sheep. Eighty-two students completed the survey and slightly more than half of them checked at least one of these items. Because I had been noticing how girls and boys seemed to be responding differently to some of the objects and activities, I wanted to look at whether or not there were also differences in the area of misconceptions. In addition, I wondered if students who stuck to these mixed images of culture and time were more likely to prefer fantasy to fact. Did they know the information but for some reason choose to ignore it? To check for this, I classified the responses to item number four according to gender and according to students' reading preference. Results of these comparisons are given in tables 5.4 and 5.5.

Misconceptions were present in 54 percent of the responses from the total group of eighty-two students. When broken down by gender, these data showed that 53 percent of the girls in the study and 48 percent of the boys included misconceptions in their responses. These figures seem reasonably close and, although no statistical analysis was conducted, it appears that for this group of students, misconceptions occur at about the same rate for boys as for girls.

There were, however, some interesting differences when misconceptions were considered in light of reading preference. Of the students who preferred to read fiction, 43 percent included misconceptions in their survey responses, as compared to only 25 percent of those who preferred nonfiction. Of the students who reported that they liked fiction and nonfiction equally, 66 percent had misconceptions on their surveys (see table 5.5).

Table 5.5.   Reading Preference and Misconceptions

Level of Understanding	Prefers Fiction	Prefers Nonfiction	Likes Fiction and Nonfiction Equally
Misconceptions	10 (43%)	3 (25%)	31 (66%)
No Misconceptions	13 (57%)	9 (75%)	16 (34%)
Total	23	12	47

When I chose to compare these data, I suspected that students who prefer nonfiction are more concerned with, and aware of, detail and factual kinds of information than are those who prefer fiction. I also suspected that the students who liked both equally well would fall somewhere in the middle of the other two groups in terms of misconceptions. My suspicion regarding a correlation between readers of nonfiction and a lower incidence of misconceptions was supported by the data. However, my assumption regarding where the fiction/nonfiction group would fit in relation to the other two groups proved to be incorrect. A statistical analysis of the data was not conducted but the differences between these groups are fairly striking.

Important to exploring the differences represented in table 5.5 is a consideration of what it means to prefer nonfiction to fiction, or to enjoy both equally. To generalize in the broadest sense, perhaps those who prefer nonfiction are more analytical and detail oriented, while the fiction readers might be considered more imaginative and freethinking. We might then ask what are the characteristics of the individual who likes fiction and nonfiction equally, which was the case for the majority of students in this project.

The first interpretation that comes to mind is that students who enjoy reading fiction and nonfiction equally are the ones most easily confused by the complexities of culture and time. Another interpretation would be that those who like to venture into the world of fact and the world of fantasy equally well are blending the two in narrative, but in an intentional and purposeful way. Would this be a narrative of confusion, or would it be one that places meaning in a more holistic frame? Consider, for example, the book, *Einstein's Dreams*, written by Alan Lightman (1993), an MIT professor who teaches physics and writing.

The book is a collection of essays by Lightman that express what he thinks Albert Einstein might have been dreaming, or reflecting on, when he was developing the general theory of relativity. In each essay, time is configured differently. In one essay, time is like a river, flowing in one direction but with streams that meander off; in another it is a circle forever to be repeated; and in still another there are two kinds of time—mechanical time and body time. The narrative Lightman weaves in each of these is exquisite and laced with multiple meanings. The question I am posing in view of this research project is, do we consider

Lightman confused? There can be no doubt on reading these essays that Lightman knows a great deal about time and at a highly abstract level. However, when he writes of time standing still, would we say he is operating under a misconception, or would we say that he is doing something different? Might we say that Lightman was playing with time and could we also say that the book lets us see how Lightman makes meaning of time?

In review, several interpretations might be offered for the persistence with culture/time mix on the follow-up surveys and for the lack of deletions on the revised concept maps. One explanation would say that students just didn't get it and that they stuck with their misconceptions throughout the unit. Another explanation is that what I am labeling as misconceptions may actually be something else. During the interviews, when I asked students about the mix of cultures and time periods, or the inclusion of stereotypes on their maps, they revealed that they were not nearly as confused as I thought they were. In most cases, children either provided a reasonable rationale, such as, "Well, the Pueblo people didn't have teepees, but they must have had some teepee-like tent for when they traveled," or they changed their work and provided the more appropriate response.

On my last visit to the classrooms, I held an open discussion with students and asked them to help me understand some things I was confused about. One of the things I asked was, "What is a teepee?" They told me that it is a kind of house or shelter that is made of hides and wood, and that it was used by Indians of the Plains. They also told me it is a home for Indians and that it is a *symbol* for Indian houses. As I brought out earlier in this chapter, these students usually did not see what I was calling a misconception as any sort of error. The lack of deletions on the concept maps at the end of the study unit would support this observation, as would the inclusion of mammoths and horses on the follow-up survey. For those students who were interviewed, the inclusion of mammoths in an illustration of ancestral Pueblo life was not problematic. Even though they could explain that the mammoths were earlier than the emergence of Puebloan culture, students seemed to think they should remain on the map.

When I gave directions for revising concept maps, I tried to be consistent with the original directions, meaning that I did not ask students to show distinct time periods for ancestral Pueblo life. One student, Crystal, raised her hand after I had finished giving directions and asked two questions: "Do you want all the time periods of Anasazi life? Can I put a mammoth in it?" I told her she should make it the way she wanted. She knew that the sanctioned version of Pueblo history did not include mammoths but she was asking my permission to include them anyway.

It would be easy to explain this mixture of culture and time as being reflective of the local geography. I could interpret these blends of time and peoples as being misconceptions that grow from the potpourri of images on the local landscape, but I am not convinced that this is what was actually happening. I believe the issues raised here are far more complex and a number of things may be going on at the same time. One facet of this problem was brought out in my earlier discussion of the students' understanding of culture. If children are given no more in the way of a definition for culture than the one that appears in textbooks like *Colorado Grassroots*—"The customs and ways of life of a group of people" (Schmidt 1989:63)—then we might expect a largely Anglo group of children to blur the lines between Navajo and Pueblo. The organizational scheme that delineates between these groups of people may have been very unclear for most of the students in this study. What teachers or anthropologists think of as culture, students may interpret as race. It is common for people to define others through difference—or how the other is different from self. The most common question Anglo children reportedly ask Native Americans is, "Are you an Indian?" or "Are you a real Indian?" The flimsy definitions we give students for complex concepts like culture may contribute, in part, to their seeming confusion. Another aspect of this problem of time/culture mix is in our own (educators) understanding of how children use images. Perhaps we need to reconsider what we are calling stereotypes. We need to look, for example, at the difference between teepee as a stereotypical image of Indians and teepee as an icon for Indian houses.

I would like to close this section on conceptual change by suggesting that the time/culture stew reflected in some of the student products collected in this study is more than the result of a confusing landscape and poor definitions. Many of the students came away from the Crow Canyon field trip with a more sophisticated understanding of culture. Even so, their expanded knowledge did not motivate most of them to change what I perceived as misconceptions. For this reason, I am proposing that what children included in the maps, the surveys, and other types of data, were critical to the way in which they were making meaning. This will be the focus of chapter 6.

Instruction and Conceptual Change

Understanding how instruction affected children's ideas about the past and contributed to their knowledge was one of the most difficult aspects of this project to explore. The concept maps were particularly useful for showing a kind of before and after perspective but provided little help in tracking changes in student thinking. Virtually all the data that related to this question came from observation or direct student questioning. Seeing change depended on thoughtful student reflection and on being in the right place at the right time. These insights happened almost exclusively during the Crow Canyon field trips and during the closing discussions I had with each class.

To review, changes in student concept maps included: elaboration on the number of examples included in the object-based categories they had created, an expansion on the number and types of categories, and an increase in the number of cross-links on their maps. The more concrete aspects of change are probably easiest to identify. The list of new objects on student maps could easily be traced to several of the Crow Canyon activities. The most frequently added objects were the atlatl, the fire-making kit, manos and metates, and gourds. Atlatls and gourds were present in two of the activities that classes participated in at Crow Canyon: Ancient Lifestyles and Windows into the Past. Children encountered the fire-making kits in three of the center's program components, and the manos and metates were included in the Simulated Dig and Lifestyles sessions. These objects did not appear in any other parts of student instruction either before or after the field trip, so it is reasonable to assume that knowledge of these objects was directly linked to instruction at Crow Canyon. It is, however, difficult to say if one of these activities contributed to student learning more than did the others. In the Lifestyles session, students actually interacted with these tools; they ground corn with manos and metates, attempted to start a fire with a bow, hearth board, and spindle stick, and threw spears using atlatls. It might well be argued that the "doing" involved in this lesson caused students to remember and integrate new knowledge more effectively. It could also be argued that students added these new objects to their construction because they encountered them in more than one place—the repetition worked to embed them in their thinking, or it could be a combination of the two—interaction and increased familiarity. Many of the other objects added to the concept maps, such as corrugated pottery and cloud blower pipes, can also be linked to particular instructional activities at Crow Canyon.

The more sophisticated changes in the maps, meaning the cross-links and the inclusion of categories that move outside basic needs, also seem to grow out of specific experiences students had on their Crow Canyon trip. Although it is more difficult to establish a direct link between some of these kinds of changes and actual events than with the more object-focused changes, I believe some connections can be seen. One small example would be of the student who added culture to his concept map (figure 5.1). Four of the topics he linked to culture were identical to those that Crow Canyon educators introduced in the Windows activity: religion, political systems, language, and traditions. These are aspects of culture that children who come to the Center do not typically identify, so the educators make a point of telling students how culture is more than what we can see and touch. The changes that related to weather, climate, and geography may be connected to the site tour of Yellow Jacket Pueblo. This is supported by the fact that I observed more of this type of change on the Dixon maps than on those from South. South students did not go on a site tour; it was the primary program difference between the two groups. During the field trip, Dixon students became actively engaged in looking at the landscape the pueblo had been situated on and in analyzing why it would have been a desirable place to live.

Although all of these students had visited a number of other sites, this trip seemed to be different for them. I was walking behind one student, Margie, during the site tour when she made the comment, "This is so much better than Mesa Verde." The girl with her agreed and they talked about why they felt this way. I had trouble hearing them, so I asked them at dinner that evening what they had meant by the comment. Margie replied, "I liked Yellow Jacket better because it is not so fixed up." She went on to tell me that she liked seeing the excavations and the ruins, and that it was different than seeing everything put back together (reconstructed) like at Mesa Verde. She also said that she liked being able to see artifacts (mostly pot sherds) on the ground and that everything at Mesa Verde was behind glass. Although she did not say so, I suspect that context also made a difference for her. At Mesa Verde, objects appear out of context in museum cases, while at Yellow Jacket it was easier for Margie to see evidence of human occupation because some of the artifacts were still in place.

Because of this conversation with Margie, I included a question about the site tour on the follow-up survey for Dixon students. I asked them how the tour of Yellow Jacket was different than a trip to Mesa Verde. The majority of them said that the big difference was not being able to see artifacts on the ground at Mesa Verde. Why this was so important to students became clearer to me when I reviewed the notes from one of the closing discussions. I asked the students if the past seemed real to them or if it seemed more like a fantasy. Their response was that this past (ancestral Pueblo) seemed real and that the past of kings and queens and "all that stuff over in England" did not seem real. When I asked why, they explained that the ancestral Pueblo past seems real because you can see evidence of it.

It seems that the aspects of instruction that made the greatest difference for these students were the educational environment they were in (archaeological sites, replica structures, simulated research areas) and the use of objects that served as a special kind of text from which they could make inferences about the past. The role that instruction, situation, and text each play in the development of student constructions will be brought out again in the next chapter.

Through the course of data collection, I realized that some of the presumptions I began with led to dead ends. I found no reason to believe that, as I had suspected originally, students who were born in the Waterville community had any greater interest in local heritage than those who had moved from other places. In addition, I concluded that some of my original ideas regarding gender differences in constructing the past were incorrect. The preference shown by both girls and boys for particular kinds of artifacts did not seem to be related to gender. On the other hand, I had no prior expectations concerning how the students would place women into the Pueblo past, but the interviews clearly showed that these children, boys and girls alike, included males in their constructions of the past far more often than females.

The primary goal of this chapter has been to present the body of data collected during the research period; these pieces of the past became my text for reading student constructions of Pueblo history. In chapter 6, I will move into a discussion of how these artifacts of my research reflect the way that the children participating in the project were making history.

Making Meaning of the Past   6

Albert and the Ninja-sazis

THE SETTING IS CAROLINE NORTON'S CLASS at South Elementary School. It is about 1:30 P.M. and Caroline's west-facing classroom is drenched in the combined glow of a warm October sun and the reflection of golden leaves dancing on the playground just outside the window. Small groups of students are moving into private areas around the room to work on an assignment from Caroline. It is an activity from the Crow Canyon pretrip packet. Each group has been given a topic to work with; included are houses, families, clothing, tools, and food. A large strip of white paper has been cut into sections to form a jigsaw puzzle. Caroline has explained that these topics are like puzzle pieces, each contributing to a culture's way of life. The task for each group is to take a piece of the puzzle and illustrate that particular topic for people living today and for the ancestral Pueblo people who lived 700 years ago. For example, students who are given the topic of food are to take a puzzle piece, draw a line through the middle, and, on one side, show the foods that they and their families eat today. The foods ancestral Pueblo people probably ate are to be drawn on the other half of the puzzle piece. When all of the puzzle pieces are completed, the group will come together and put them into place.

I decide to follow the group that has "Tools" as their topic. It is comprised of four boys who seem to be under the leadership of the smallest one, a boy I will refer to as Albert. I give them a few minutes to get things on paper without my intrusion. When I approach, I find they are each absorbed in drawing what I presume are tools. Not being able to identify what a number of the objects are, my eyes wander to the top of the page. This is when I first realize that the topic of tools has gone through some sort of metamorphosis and the title of their puzzle piece now reads "Weapons." I examine the two sides of the puzzle in search of the comparison between the different time periods and cultures. I soon realize that I am seeing virtually the same objects on both sides of the puzzle piece. It is at this point that I decide to ask for help and begin quizzing the group, "What are these?" (I am pointing to round discs that have a kind of rough or jagged edge. They faintly resemble saw blades.) Albert informs me, with fairly obvious impatience, that they are Ninja throwing stars.

Thinking that there is a problem with group dynamics and that each boy is simply drawing what he likes, where he likes, I ask: "Did the Anasazi use throwing stars?" I am surprised to hear their quick response, "Well, they probably had something like that." The boys work to move me quickly past what I am trying to point out is an inaccuracy in their work. It becomes quite clear to me that my input is not welcome. I make another attempt saying, "I see that you have the word 'weapons' written as your title; weren't you supposed to be working on 'tools?' Are all tools weapons?" In their reply, they reinforce the earlier message—that I am not helping. They tell me, "Well, a lot of them are the same."

I feel that I have pushed my point as far as is useful and move away from the group to circulate around the room. When I return to them later, I find that they have scratched through the word "weapons" and replaced it with "tools." I also see that a few of the former Ninja weapons have been scratched out. I am not sure that I am happy with what has happened. As a researcher, I felt that my prodding might get them to clarify their choices to me. I realize that I have, instead, caused them to censor their work.

At the end of the small group work, the class reconvenes to share what they have accomplished thus far. When they get to the tools/weapons group, Albert speaks as their leader. He points to the various objects and identifies them, including the Ninja throwing stars—even the ones that were crossed out. Caroline has the same response that I have had and seizes the moment to question their choices. She asks of the class, "Are Ninjas and Anasazis same?" To my utter amazement, the majority of the class replies with a strong, heart-felt, "Well yeah—kind of." The look on Caroline's face reflects my own confusion. She continues to question the class. "How are they (Ninjas and Anasazi) alike?" The list of common traits the students create includes style of dress (both groups wear belted, loose, cotton clothing) and tools or weapons. Several students help Albert support his position, adding that both Ninjas and Anasazis might have spears. Caroline does not challenge their perceptions, nor does she comment on them. After the class has finished commenting, she moves to the next group of students and on with the lesson.

I wasn't quite sure what I had just witnessed but I knew it was important. After school that day, Caroline and I discussed the possibilities, but had to admit that we did not have a clue as to how or why the students were making these connections. It seemed to me that whatever it was, it was connected to that larger question I had wanted to get at: "How do children construct the past and how do they make meaning of it?" Because the children seemed to have no difficulty understanding one another, and because Caroline and I had great difficulty seeing their point of view, I felt that we were outsiders. We could not see what they saw because it was part of a child's construction and it made sense in a child's world—Caroline and I simply could not get it. I decided that I needed to see more than just the analogies the kids were making, I needed to understand more than why Albert saw similarities between Ninjas and Anasazi; I needed to know why he selected Ninjas rather than some other group of people. The other students were able to see Albert's reasoning, but didn't come up with the Ninja idea themselves. I felt that exploring these issues might give me insight into the ways that individual children construct the past and, perhaps, information regarding any patterns that might exist. To get at these issues, I decided to talk with an authority: I would ask Albert.

I Just Do It That Way

My interview with Albert took place on the morning after the Ninja-sazi saga. During the first part of our talk, I followed the interview guide closely. I learned that Albert had always lived in Waterville, that his father was born there, and that he lived with his grandmother. He said that science was his favorite subject because he liked to try new things and that he liked to read chapter books, particularly mysteries. When I asked him where he would go if he had a time machine, he said to Anasazi times and that maybe he would be hunting. When I asked why, he said it was because you might get to use a bow and arrow. He said that he had shot a bow and arrow before and that his father hunts. At this point, I decided to ask about the Ninja-sazis:

> Elaine: When your class divided into work groups yesterday, I believe you were in the tool group. (*Albert cuts in.*)
>
> Albert: Tools and weapons.
>
> Elaine: OK, tools and weapons. Anyway, Ms. Norton asked the kids if Ninja's and Anasazis were alike and they all said "sort of." What do you think they meant by that?
>
> Albert: That they (Anasazi) used weapons like them (Ninjas).
>
> Elaine: So, do you think their weapons were the same?
>
> Albert: Sort of.

Elaine: How do you think Ninja and Anasazi culture would be different?

Albert: Ninjas dress in black.

Elaine: OK, how about real and fantasy, are they both fantasy?

Albert: Huh uh (*no*). The Indians are not fantasy because they lived a long time ago.

Elaine: But the Ninjas are fiction? (*This is where I realize I have not understood Albert's concept of Ninjas, I was thinking of cartoon Ninjas.*)

Albert: Hu-uh (*no*).

Elaine: Ok, Albert, I confess that I don't know much about Ninjas—teach me.

Albert: Ninja is a special way of fighting, it's kind of like karate.

Elaine: So they are both real, but the Anasazi was a group of people that lived a long time ago and Ninjas are people living now that take Ninja training?

Albert: Yeah (*he pauses and seems to be thinking*), but you know how Anasazi have them blow gun thingees? Ninjas have them too. (*This is interesting; to my knowledge the ancestral Pueblo people did not use blowguns. I pointed this out to Caroline's class the day before when the question was raised during the presentation by the tool/weapons group.*)

Elaine: Oh, I remember we talked about that yesterday. Have you found some information that says they used blowguns?

Albert: Um-um, no. Tony just said that he saw it in a movie.

At this point, I decided to leave the Ninja-sazis alone and move to the other questions. Albert said he thought that Anasazi culture changed over time and that they did things differently over the years, such as the way they built their houses, and the way they hunted. When I asked him how he knew that things changed, he said that now we use guns to hunt and people used to use bow and arrow, his rationale was that if things change now they would have back then as well. I then asked him to contrast life now with life at Mesa Verde when people lived there:

Albert: It would be harder then because they had to hunt for food and make houses and move. Like the Plains Indians had to move their teepees and that's where they lived, in teepees.

Elaine: Did the Anasazi have teepees?

Albert: Huh-uh (*no*).

Albert talked a little more about Plains Indians and how life would have been hard for them. I then brought out the concept map he had drawn and began to ask him questions about it:

Elaine: This is your concept map and I wanted to be sure I could understand things the way you meant them. Let's look at the first category, you have transportation and (*pointing to the links he has created*) you are saying they walked, and is this word horse?

Albert: That's horse.

Elaine: OK, so the Anasazi had horses?

Albert: Yeah (*slight pause*), or they didn't but the Plains Indians did.

Elaine: But this is a concept map of (*pause*)?

Albert: Anasazi. (*Albert has a broad grin on his face and his next statement comes with great clarity and confidence.*) But I just do it that way!

When we came to teepees on his concept map, he told me that they belonged with Plains Indians. I asked him why he put it on the Anasazi map and he replied, "Because that is part of Indians." His answer was similar to an explanation given during my closing discussion with one of the classes: "Teepees stand for Indian houses."

When I brought out the artifacts for the storytelling portion of the interview (see appendix 2), I found that Albert could identify all of them. He was even able to tell me that the rock included in the set of artifacts was used for grinding. Without hesitation, Albert selected the projectile point, or arrowhead as he referred to it, as the starter for his story. When I asked him to tell a story about the arrowhead, I was surprised to hear his very literal beginning and to discover that I would have to continually question him to keep the story going. Throughout the story, I continued to prompt Albert with questions like, "What happened next?" or "Can you tell me anything else?" His story, which follows, was actually quite brief:

The Indian made it (the arrowhead) with another rock (*he demonstrates*) like that. He was Anasazi, about thirty-seven years old. He was real careful. He made it sharp. He put it on a spear and threw it at a deer. He killed the deer and ate the meat, and shared some of it with his tribe. He cut the deer up with a knife, a bone knife. After the deer died, he took the arrowhead out and saved it because they were hard to make.

The story was not what I had expected. Albert had been so caught up in his Ninja version of Anasazi life that I fully expected his story to revolve around it. Instead, he gave me the nonfiction version. Throughout my conversations and interview with Albert, I was continually questioning and challenging his beliefs. I wanted to clarify what Albert actually knew about Anasazi life so I could differentiate between misconceptions and a more intentional creativity with factual information. This process, admittedly, caused Albert to begin censoring what he told me, but it was essential to determining whether the Ninja-sazis and the mix of postcontact Plains and precontact Pueblo cultures grew out of misinformation or if they were an expression of something else. I would have been reluctant to do this with other students, those who seemed less sure of their own ideas. My goal was not to change anyone's ideas, so it was important to work with a student like Albert who defended and stubbornly stuck to his own story.

In the end, I felt that Albert chose not to give me his story when I asked for it. It may be that I had worn him down and he made the decision to give me a more scholarly story, or it could be that withholding his story was an oppositional act. I would say that Albert did give his story in the concept map, in the tools/weapons activity, and in much of the interview. His story was a collage of past and present, of Plains Indians, Ninjas, and Anasazi. He had created a tapestry from these elements that he found meaning in. It was a story he was intrigued by and that he delighted in.

The picture he painted was not formed from hazy ideas and misinformation—Albert knew that the Anasazi did not have horses, that they did not live in teepees, and that they were Indians who lived a long time ago. And, as I soon learned, he had a far clearer understanding of Ninjas than I did. When asked, he could provide the facts quite clearly, but his preference was to build his own narrative from these various stories. When Albert smiled at me during the interview and with exasperation said, "I just do it that way," I was reminded of a similar encounter I once had with another little boy. I was talking with a friend's five-year-old son, Christopher, about a frog he had just caught. I asked him what he planned to do with the frog and he said, "I'm going to take it to school to scare girls with." I pointed out that some girls are not scared of frogs. On hearing this, Christopher's face grew stormy and in a firm low voice he said, "I like for girls to be scared of frogs." In both cases, the boys were telling me that I was trying to rewrite their story and that they really were not in favor of my changes.

Through the interview, I was able to learn what Albert knew of the Pueblo past but I was left with questions concerning why he chose to use the information as he did. I wasn't clear why he chose to focus on weapons and Ninjas but I suspected that it had something to do with Albert himself. I wondered how much the saga of the Ninga-sazis was actually about Albert. To explore issues of personal identity in student constructions of the past, I examined the narratives of the other children who were interviewed.

Telling Stories

Telling a story on the spur of the moment is not something most of us are comfortable with. The children in this study were no different than adults in this respect. While they all did offer something in the way of a story, several of them prefaced theirs with, "It's hard for me to make up stories." In all four cases where children were most adamant about this—Albert's included—the stories told were literal accounts of how the artifact would have been made or used. These children were giving me what might be considered the legitimized stories; they consisted of information that might be given to them in a classroom. They were school stories, not the narratives created by children. With the other eleven students, all the stories had imaginative elements and only one of them required a significant amount of prompting from me. In each case, prompts were only used when the student came to a long pause, yet didn't seem finished with the story. The prompts were questions like, "What happened next?" or "Then what happened?"

Of all the objects I had for students to examine, the only ones not chosen for stories were the pottery sherds. Five students selected the projectile point as a focus for their stories, four of them selected the mug, three students chose to tell a story about the yucca sandal, two selected the atlatl, and one told a story about the mano. In selecting the artifacts, I attempted to provide a mix of what might be interpreted as boy-things or girl-things. In the end, this did not seem to be important. The most commonly chosen objects—the mug and the point—were selected by both girls and boys. The gender difference that did appear in the narratives had to do with story characters. The main characters in eleven of the fifteen stories were male, three were female, and one child told a story about Indians that made no reference to gender. I was surprised by these results, especially considering that nine of the interviewees were female and six were male. Two girls and one boy told the three stories about females. It may be that children find it easier to imagine males than females in Native American history. Much of the literature on North American history, including juvenile literature, has emphasized the roles of men and said little about women and children. It may also be that children of either sex have difficulty imagining historical roles for women because they have so few models to work from. Other researchers have made similar observations regarding children's images of the past:

> We are concerned about girls' tendency, particularly when illustrating textbook like passages, to depict a past inhabited by fewer women than men. But we are equally concerned about boys' tendency to depict a past inhabited almost exclusively by men. . . . If these patterns suggest that girls view the past with less than 20-20 vision, then boys are blind in one eye. [Wineburg 2001:129]

The stories created by the children all seemed to involve similar themes, with the two most common themes having to do with parent and child interaction, and technological innovation. The four stories that did not fit these themes conveyed more unique ideas. One story was about persistence and fulfilling a task, another might be considered a tragedy, one of the stories was action packed, and another was explanatory in nature. In the one I am calling explanatory, a character was created and a simple plot established, but the purpose of the story seemed to be to convey information. In this case, the girl telling the story, Kari, was concerned with the mug's construction and felt that it would not be good to drink from. The girl in Kari's story used the cup only for cold water and did not heat anything in it.

Following are three of the stories I have selected from the fifteen. I chose the stories told by Crystal, Ricky, and Randy because they each gave their story willingly, without prompts from me. Thus, these stories seem to convey children's voices more fully than do those where more questions were needed. I also selected them because they are, in many ways, particularly in terms of theme and essence, prototypical of stories told by other children. Prior to each story is a short biographical sketch of the storyteller. These descriptions are limited by the amount of contact I had with each child and by her or his openness to me.

Crystal

Crystal was a tall, blonde, healthy-looking fourth grader. I noticed her the first time I walked into her classroom because of her rather unique footwear. She was wearing a pair of high-heeled, see-through sandals that appeared to be constructed of some kind of heavy rubber. She stood out from the other girls because her shoes were so different; they were actually dangerous looking. The heels were probably higher than any I had ever worn and I wondered why anyone would put herself at risk in this way. I could not imagine Crystal being able to maneuver on the playground wearing these stilt-like shoes.

During the interview, Crystal told me that her favorite subjects were math, spelling, and reading. Like other fourth-grade girls, she was heavily into books such as *The Babysitters' Club*. When I first asked if she liked to learn about the past she said, "Yes, It's pretty fun cause it's different than how we live now. Like back then they had (pause) they didn't have shoes that much, so it must have been hard. They must have had hard feet." She went on to tell me that her mom was from California and her dad was from Texas. Crystal said that her favorite way to learn about the past was to visit places where people lived a long time ago. She said, "You could ask questions about how people did things, what kind of clothes they wore and if they had separate tribes." When I asked her where she would go if she could travel into the past, she chose to be in a deep canyon where she could walk barefoot and be able to find things to live off of. She seemed to think that men and women might have different kinds of work and that boys would help their dads, and girls would help their moms. She believed that Pueblo people changed over time; some of her comments regarding change were given in chapter 5. Crystal was able to identify all the artifacts I placed before her, although she was hesitant about the atlatl. When I asked her to select one of the objects to tell a story about, she chose the yucca sandal. Her narrative follows:

> Once there were these sandals and they were just laying around and the Anasazi didn't have any shoes or anything to wear on their feet. One of the Anasazi walked by and he said, "I wonder what that is." He stopped and put his foot in it and said, "Wow, this would work out for something to cover my feet." He ran back to the village and told everybody that he found this new pair of shoes. They said, "How did you make them?" He said, "Well I didn't really make them, I found them but I know how to make them." So he gathered all the stuff to make them and started weaving them and then set them in the sun to dry. The next day they were dry, so there was a pair for one of the women. He became kind of like a businessman and almost everyone in the village had a pair of shoes except for one person. He didn't like that person very much but he decided that since he made them for everyone else, it would be pretty mean not to make him (the guy he didn't like) some. So he started making some, they weren't the best shoes but they worked. (*Crystal pauses and laughs.*) Then everybody noticed that it was hard to keep the sandals on, so he said, "I can make them fit better but I will need to measure your foot." So he made everybody some little strings that helped the sandals stay on better. Then they said, "This feels kind of rough on my feet." So he took some rocks and ground them into sand and filled the sandals up. Then everyone said, "This feels much better." Then the man said, "OK, I hope there's no more problem with the shoes." But someone said, "This shoe is too small for me because my feet go past the end." So then he had to make like a whole new pair. He had to grind up all the sand, he had to make the string, and then he had a pair. Then, there was a baby that was just born. He said, "I wonder how I can make a baby shoe." So he took all his stuff to make a big shoe and tried making a baby one. Well, it worked. He put them on the baby and it was practically walking.

Ricky

Ricky was one of the most verbal students I interviewed. He was a handsome, athletic-looking boy with dark eyes and hair. His favorite subjects were science and geography—especially geography. He said that he really liked to travel, which was why he found geography interesting. During the previous summer he had gone to Alaska with his grandmother; they had visited Anchorage, Denali, Fairbanks, Valdez, and Whittier. He told me they saw nineteen grizzly bears and seven black bears. Ricky said that his grandmother had been to China three times and that she had just returned from Guatemala. He said she had been to Greece as well. It was obvious that geography excited him: "In my new room, I'm gonna have this U.S.

map and I'm gonna have a map of Colorado and I'm gonna try to climb all the fourteeners (mountains over 14,000 feet in elevation) before I die." Ricky told me that history bored him, but that it was his family's favorite subject. He said he mostly read nonfiction but that he was currently reading *Gulliver's Travels*, which he identified as fiction. He reported that his favorite fiction books told stories from Europe and around the world. Ricky said that his mom was born in Colorado and his dad was born in Kansas. If he could choose, he said his favorite period in history to visit would be World War II. Ricky said military aircraft and aircraft carriers intrigued him. He also said he would never want to be a pilot because his grandfather had been killed while testing the F-14. Ricky had read about evolution but wasn't sure exactly how much earlier the origin of modern humans would have been than the time when the ancestral Pueblo people lived. Ricky seemed primed to tell a story for me; he said that Crystal told him I would ask for a story. He chose to tell about the projectile point:

> I pick the arrowhead. Should I start? (*I tell him yes.*) Back in the Anasazi age, there was this little girl. She went on a walk and found an arrowhead that had fallen off somebody's spear. So, she went back to Mesa Verde and she showed it to everybody. When nobody claimed it, she decided to keep it. She took it out to where she had found it and buried it. She went home and went to sleep. When she woke up the next morning, she went out to see if it was still there. It wasn't and she walked back and told her parents that it was gone. They went to help her look for it and they found it. She had not dug deep enough. Her father took the arrowhead and put it on a spear for her. Now she practices throwing the spear from the spot where she found it (the arrowhead).

I told Ricky that I really liked his story and asked him why he chose to tell about a girl. He said that a boy would have done something different. When I asked him to explain, he said, "Well, I don't think a boy would have found it, he would have made it. He would have hunted with it and he might have lost it in a buffalo. That would have been bad because they might have been saving it for a ceremony." I asked him if the little girl in his story might have used the spear her father made for hunting. Ricky said, "I don't think girls were allowed to hunt back then, well, that's what I've read. Girls did like the cooking and stuff, but I don't think that was right. My old (former) teacher hunts and I went hunting with her and her daughter and husband. I think that the girls should have been able to hunt."

Randy

Randy's favorite subjects were science and art. He was particularly enthusiastic when he spoke of art and the art projects he had been involved in at school. He reported that he was an A+ art student. Like Ricky, Randy also talked of hunting. He said that he hunts elk with his dad but that he cannot actually shoot the gun because he is too young. He said that he will have to take lessons (I believe this is required by law in Colorado) but he has to wait until he is twelve years old. In the meantime, he said, he and his dad target practice using his dad's pistol. Randy chose to tell a story about the atlatl:

> There was this kid who was trying to learn how to use an atlatl. He tried and tried but he couldn't hit anything. He went to his father to ask for help. His father gave him lessons and he tried and tried and tried but he still couldn't hit anything. Then his father decided to hire someone to give him lessons, but he was still no good. The kid tried to shoot some other things; he learned to use the bow and arrow, and got to go hunting with his dad. Finally he went hunting with the atlatl but he didn't get anything. His dad said, "I guess the atlatl is just not your thing."

Randy was somewhat less verbal than other children I had interviewed, so I was pleasantly surprised when he offered his story without a lot of prompting. He considered his words carefully and turned the atlatl over and over in his hands as he talked. He spoke slowly but consistently and when he finally came to a stop, it was clear that he was finished.

My initial reaction to these three stories, as well as many of the others, was how closely they mirrored something important in the lives of the storytellers. The issues children chose to focus on might not be considered significant to others but were, I believe, important to them. Crystal is a little girl who thinks a lot about feet and shoes, and she selected the sandal as a springboard for her story. Her interview was filled with references to shoes and, from my observations, she seemed to use shoes to express her own uniqueness. It seems reasonable to say that "funky" shoes were an important part of her identity at the time she was involved in this research project. Ricky and Randy were preadolescent boys growing up in southwest Colorado. In this part of the world, hunting is not a novelty; it is a common practice in many local families, particularly for males. Both of these boys had been involved in the activity with their fathers and friends for a year or more and, as Randy pointed out, were approaching the age at which they will be allowed to hunt on their own. Ricky emphasized the fact that he thought women and girls should be able to hunt but that he did not think they had been allowed to do so in Anasazi times. In keeping with his belief, he gave the little girl in his story a spear but he didn't let her hunt with it.

Constructing the Past

A Framework for Understanding

Before discussing how the students in this project were constructing the past, I would first like to provide a framework for viewing the kinds of choices that learners make on the path to the construction of meaning. This framework is based on some fundamental assumptions that I am making. The first of these is that, from a constructivist perspective, the human mind is a meaning-making organism. The learner is driven to make sense of the world, to construct understanding out of the information that she or he encounters. A second assumption is that a constructivist frame has not been the theoretical foundation on which American education rests. I believe that this is as true for informal education settings, such as museums, as it is for public schools.

American education has, instead, been grounded in a model of knowledge transmission where learners are expected to ingest and reproduce information that comes from authoritative sources. In this transmission model, successful learners are those who can most closely reproduce the information in its original form. Of this traditional approach to education, constructivists might say that learners use the information to create meaning for themselves but that their understanding may not mirror that of the authority. The framework that I am proposing here to show how learners make meaning of information about the past accepts this position but puts forth another possibility—the possibility that personal understanding is not reached and that meaning is, thus, not made. A final assumption is that there are two fundamental ways in which knowledge is structured: logical-scientific thinking and narrative thinking (Bruner 1996:39). The framework rests on the belief that a learner's view of the nature of knowledge and of her/his role in the construction of knowledge are critical to the making of meaning (figure 6.1).

This framework includes six learner types that are derived from one's perspective on the nature of knowledge, the level of knowledge proficiency achieved, and the way in which knowledge is structured. I want to clarify that when I say that the learner understands that knowledge is constructed, I don't mean that she or he could necessarily articulate this. What I am trying to convey is that such learners recognize that they are capable of thinking. They question, they explore, they create theories. They do not simply memorize and accept information; they have a reciprocal relationship with the subject matter. A brief description of the six learner types follows:

TYPE A Type A learners understand that they are active participants in the construction of knowledge. They can transfer learning from one situation to another. The learner structures knowledge of the past in terms of meaningful events (narrative). Attention is given to essences or overarching themes. Narratives are more likely to reflect issues of greater social significance rather than themes that only have meaning for the individual. Example: The student who creates a work of historic fiction that is well researched and that presents the complexities of life in the past.

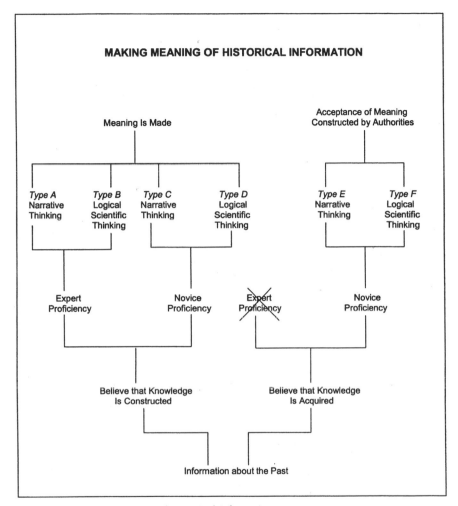

Figure 6.1.   Making Meaning of Historical Information

TYPE B Type B learners understand that they are active participants in the construction of knowledge. They can transfer learning from one situation to another. This learner structures the past chronologically and exhibits historical thinking, with attention given to evidence, causality, and relationships. Type B learners view past events in complex ways and recognize that multiple perspectives may exist. Example: This learner would approach information about the past in much the same way that a professional historian or archaeologist would approach it.

TYPE C Type C learners understand that they are active participants in the construction of knowledge and they can transfer learning to new situations. Type C learners structure the past in terms of personally meaningful themes; the themes may also be relevant to others in their cultural peer group. Type C learners may have a fairly strong understanding of related factual information but are comfortable with sacrificing accuracy in order to achieve the thematic goal of the narrative. This learner will often provide a rationale in support of her or his choices. He or she may be a very flexible thinker and can possibly move back and forth between Type C and Type D. In some cases, the learner may even switch between Type C and Type B, depending on their proficiency with the information. This switching may occur as the result of specific cues given by an authority regarding the kind of understanding that is appropriate for the situation. Example: A student who creates romanticized stories about life in the antebellum South but who can pass a test on the harsh realities of slavery that the plantation system depended on. Albert, from the southwest Colorado case study, would be an example of a type C learner.

TYPE D Type D learners understand that they are active participants in the construction of knowledge. Type D learners structure their view of the past around information they accept as evidence. They build an understanding of the past based on available evidence but they may be confused about the evidence or have incomplete information. They struggle for a sound logical view of the past and they draw from many sources. Type D learners may also have difficulty recognizing the lenses through which they view the past. Example: A learner who views a museum exhibit and draws an inaccurate understanding of the meaning of the exhibit because she or he has misinterpreted some of the information and may have constructed some misconceptions.

Note: According to this framework, Type E and Type F learners do not construct meaning in their understanding of the past but, instead, accept the meanings constructed by authoritative sources. Even though they may be seen as having a strong knowledge base, they do not achieve expert proficiency because they do not readily transfer learning to new situations.

TYPE E Type E learners believe that knowledge is something that exists outside of self. They see scholarship as the acquisition of knowledge constructed by authorities. Their primary mode of learning is memorization. The learner understands the past by memorizing and reproducing accepted narratives without questioning them. Example: A student who memorizes and accepts without question the canonical narratives of a nation.

TYPE F Type F learners believe that knowledge is something that exists outside of self. They see scholarship as the acquisition of knowledge constructed by authorities and are very adept at learning information perceived as factual. Type F learners accept narratives constructed by others and can likely provide many details to support the narrative. These details are those that are provided by authorities as evidence, not information that the student has constructed. Type F students generally achieve great success in traditional classrooms and are motivated by grades. They are likely to reject information that contradicts the canonical information they have memorized. They tend to feel threatened by situations that cause them to doubt the soundness of their approach to scholarship. These students may be very successful in school until they are asked to think for themselves. Example: The honors history student who stubbornly sticks with historical information from school textbooks even when she or he encounters information of a contradictory nature. She or he will stay rooted in her or his beliefs unless forced to move through conceptual change.

Student Constructions of the Pueblo Past

The most pervasive aspect of the way students in this research project were using information about the past is that they chose to become active agents in making sense of that information—they chose the path that leads to the making of meaning. There are several good explanations for this. To begin, as Rosenzweig and Thelen have recognized (1998), people want to play an active role in interpreting the past. A past that is not mediated by others is more intellectually exciting and personally fulfilling than a canonized history constructed by authorities. Although Rosenzweig and Thelen conducted their study with adults, I believe it is not irresponsible to assume that children hold the same views.

A second explanation for why the students in this project chose to become active agents in constructing the past is that they had had little exposure to "school history" and did not feel the need to reproduce information given to them by authorities in order to pass a test. For elementary school students, history is a subject area that is freer of the constraints imposed by more rigid curricula that are in place for subjects like mathematics and reading. Because of the emphasis on achievement in these other areas, students are likely to view them as more serious subjects because they are held accountable for them on report cards. It seems reasonable to say that the students in this project probably viewed history as a more informal area of study and, thus, felt more comfortable with their own ability to think about it without being penalized.

A final but highly important explanation for why students in the study chose to construct their own meaning of the Pueblo past rather than reproduce the constructions of others, lies in the instructional methods they experienced in their unit of study. Although instruction varied from class to class, all students had exposure to the content through a variety of different methods. Particularly significant was the use of inquiry learning that all of the students experienced at the Crow Canyon Archaeological Center. While there, students were provided with different kinds of evidence and allowed to mediate their own understandings. All of the teachers involved in the project valued critical thinking and designed activities that engaged students in the kinds of thinking that are essential to constructing historical understanding, such as observation, inference, and the recognition of assumptions.

Another common characteristic of the way that students in this project used information about the past is the way in which they chose to structure their knowledge. In reference to the Framework for Making Meaning of Historical Information (figure 6.1), the majority of the students in the study were, most of the time, operating as Type C learners. A number of them moved fluidly between Type C and Type D, and several of them, Albert in particular, occasionally spanned the gap between Types C and B. Most students only chose a logical-scientific approach to the structure of knowledge (Types B and D) when they felt that it was required.

Although with Albert, the decision to provide a fact-based story about the arrowhead rather than a more personal narrative may have even been an oppositional act. When I badgered him regarding the accurateness of some of his responses on the concept map, he stuck to his own narrative of Ninja-like Anasazis, but when I actually asked for a story, he gave me a toneless set of factual information that was loosely tied together in story form. When Crystal asked if she could put a mammoth in the final version of her concept map, she was trying to understand whether or not her personal narrative was appropriate, or if the linear construction of the past that places Pueblo people in the Four Corners long after the last mammoths died out would be better. Ricky, who had read about evolution but was somewhat confused by the vast amount of time involved, is probably one of the few students in the study who preferred the logical-scientific approach to the structure of knowledge. He loved factual information and sought it out. Because he is so bright and such an avid reader, he sometimes selected sources that may have been a little too advanced for him and he was not able to gain an accurate understanding of the information presented. Ricky liked to construct the past in a factual way but his misconceptions worked to impede this goal (Type D).

What is it about narrative that so many of these students found compelling? Why would they prefer a narrative structure to a logical-scientific organization of historical information? I believe the answer lies in what one is able to accomplish with each of the two structures. One is more suited for telling what something is about, the other for describing the condition of things. Narrative is a tool for interpretation—for the expression of meanings, whereas logical-scientific thinking is a tool for explanation, for telling what happened or how things work. Narrative provides adults and children alike with a way to make the past meaningful to their lives in the present.

Narrative might be an even more important device for children than for adults in terms of structuring information about the past. Rosenzweig and Thelen found that, to a surprising degree, people are very interested in the human past. They also found that the adults in their study exhibited a strong desire to connect with the past on a personal level and to use that connection to bring the past into the present. This would be a difficult thing for children to do because history is not about children. Even the archaeological information that the children were presented with in this study was from the world of adults. As I alluded to in the opening paragraph of chapter 1, it is a significant thing to look at the human past and not be able to find something of one's self there.

Within narrative is the flexibility to introduce themes that are important in ones own world; narrative can be true of life without being true to life. Narratives organize and contextualize information. In a narrative account of the past, the essence of the event may be more important than the details of that event. To clarify, I will draw from a familiar example, the celebration of the Nativity by Christians around the world. This sacred story of Christ's birth is reenacted in churches and communities across the globe, and is portrayed in Christian homes through the display of the crèche. In addition to Mary, Joseph, and the baby Jesus, the scene usually includes shepherds, angels, farm animals, and three kings or wise men. However, according to Biblical accounts, the three kings had to travel a long distance and did not actually see the Christ child until much later. In addition, the men are usually not identified as kings but as magi (magicians or, perhaps, astrologers). This information is generally known and accepted by Christians, yet Christmas pageants and nativity displays persistently place three kings in Bethlehem on the night of Jesus' birth. Perhaps this is because the real story for Christians is not so much about the details as it is about a holy event of such magnitude that it brought everyone together, from humble shepherds to great kings. This is the story that has meaning for Christians, and the inclusion of three kings in the Nativity is essential for conveying that meaning. For them, the essence of the story is more important than the accurate timing of events. Or, to use Albert's words, they just do it that way.

Although I am labeling the students' constructions of the Pueblo past as narratives, I am not claiming that I fully understand what their narratives were about because, in most cases, I was only able to gain a partial view. To reiterate, Albert did not seem to want to give me full access to his narrative of the Ninja-sazis, nor did he want to give it to his teacher, Caroline. However, it appears that he in some way shared it with many of his peers in the class. I am not saying that this was intentional on his part but rather, an assumption. And, I would like to add, an assumption that proved to be accurate, as evidenced by the support he drew from class members during his presentation of the Ninja-sazi weapons. The meanings that are conveyed through narrative rely on a culturally shared symbol system. It seems possible that the fourth graders in Caroline's classroom clearly understood Albert's association between Anasazis and Ninjas because they shared an understanding of the symbol system. Caroline and I were not part of the peer culture that Albert and the other fourth graders belonged to, which made it difficult for us to understand what the narrative was about or why anyone would see similarities between Ninjas and Anasazis.

Conclusion

The central point that I want to stress here is that making meaning of historical information is a choice, one that I would hope all teachers and scholars of the human past would want learners to make. This may feel like a risky proposition because it means sharing authority for interpretation. The alternative, however, is to not make meaning of the past, but to simply memorize and recite the meanings that others have made. As an educator, I would argue that the latter option involves little learning and perhaps no real thinking at all. There may be some security and satisfaction in seeing the past rendered from the lips of others exactly as we have presented it to them, but the scary truth is that this sort of knowledge is worth very little. It is, in general, not remembered for very long and is not transferable to other situations because it was not arrived at through inquiry but received in an unthinking, unquestioning manner. This sort of knowledge about the past will not lead to the preservation of historic and archaeological sites or material culture. It will not expand our understanding of what it means to be human and it will do little to elevate the scholarly study of the past to a place of public importance because it is a kind of knowledge that is borrowed, not owned. Very few people become passionate about that which is borrowed. For people to truly be able to hear the past speak to the present and inform the future, they have to be active agents in the construction of the past.

Some narratives of the past are "righter" than others due to the accuracy of the information from which they are constructed or because they are better contextualized—they render transparent the perspective of the storyteller. However, constructing responsible narratives requires practice. Those who teach about the human past must become committed to the development of educational experiences that provide this practice and that nurture its growth.

TEACHING A HISTORY THAT MATTERS

III

Constructing Pedagogy: Applying Research to Practice

7

> *A meaningful connection to the past demands, above all, active engagement. It demands imagination and empathy, so that we can fathom worlds unlike our own, contexts far from those we know, ways of thinking and feeling that are alien to us. We must do this with curiosity and respect. When we do this, the rewards are considerable.*
>
> (GERDA LERNER 1997:201)

The Transfer of Learning

IN CHAPTER 6 I INTRODUCED A FRAMEWORK for understanding how people use information about the past and how they might make meaning of it. This framework also recognizes that individuals may do something else with the information and that they might not make meaning of it at all. The problem is rooted in the transfer of learning or, rather, the lack of it. According to the framework, when information is stored and repeated, but never applied, the learner remains at the novice level. Ironically, this is what often happens with information gained through educational research. It remains a discrete, static body of work that operates independently of educational practice. Does the blame lie with researchers for not making their work more accessible to educators? Does it lie with legislators, politicians, and bureaucrats for burying educators under a mountain of standards, procedures, and accountability; or should educators carry the blame because they are, after all, the gatekeepers? Even in informal education settings there is, in many cases, a disconnect between what researchers understand about best practices and the work of the educators in those settings. A lack of funding is sometimes given as the reason for not implementing research findings, particularly in private and not-for-profit settings.

All of these explanations and countless others likely contribute to the difficulty with closing the gap between educational research and practice. Change is difficult and institutional change is even more so. History education in the United States might be viewed as an institution. It is one that typically garners little attention until someone tries to change it then, it seems, all hell breaks loose. The history wars that arose over the writing of the National History Standards are emblematic of this sensitivity to change where history is concerned, as is the sometimes heated response to museum interpretations of the past. When the Smithsonian tried to display a fiftieth-anniversary exhibit on the *Enola Gay* and the atomic bomb that was dropped on Hiroshima, powerful lobbies such as the American Legion and the Air Force Association convinced Congress to remove the display before it was shown to the public. The display that took its place was far less controversial and avoided any discussion of the consequences of nuclear warfare.

The point that I want to emphasize here and that I have tried to make throughout this book is that education about the human past needs to undergo a transformation. As Gerda Lerner states, "A meaningful connection to the past demands, above all, active engagement" (1997:201). Active engagement has not been the hallmark of history education in the United States, but it can be. And if it is, as Lerner asserts, the rewards are considerable. The risks involved in not doing so are equally considerable, as was brought out in the beginning of this book; history and power are intimately connected. Selective memory and the distortion of history are tools of oppression (Lerner 1997:206). It is only through active intellectual engagement with the past that learners, young or old, are able to build their own understandings and think critically regarding the constructions of others.

In this chapter, I will discuss how the essential understandings regarding the learning of history that were put forth in parts I and II, relate to the development of a historical pedagogy. In chapter 8, I will show how we might implement these pedagogical understandings in both formal and informal education settings. The closing chapter will look at useful methods and tools for assessing the learning of history and examining the meaning-making process.

Limited by Assumptions

When educators make assumptions regarding the learner's ability to process information about the past, boundaries are imposed on what might be learned. On the other hand, not making any kind of assumptions regarding cognitive development can result in an educational experience that is confusing or inappropriate. Somewhere between these two extremes, educators must discover how to present information about the past to young people in a way that is comprehensible but not overly simplified. To illustrate, the students in the southwestern Colorado case study were far more knowledgeable of the Pueblo past than I had expected at the beginning of the project. However, the range of their understanding was fairly narrow. Their knowledge of objects and things was extensive but their knowledge of concepts was far shallower. I believe that, to a great extent, what the children were able to learn was constrained by assumptions imposed on the instructional process by their educators. I use the term educator here to refer to myself, the teachers involved in the project, and to the larger educational community. These assumptions relate most specifically to issues of communication within the classroom and to assumptions regarding conceptual and cognitive development.

The assumptions we hold when we develop instructional activities or design a research project establish the boundaries for these endeavors. We assume that children mix time periods because they don't understand change or because they are confused and we are frustrated by our unsuccessful attempts to place their images of the past on a time line. We assume that children can only comprehend the concrete aspects of culture, such as food and shelter but are disappointed when these clues have not helped them distinguish between past and present cultures or between different groups of Native Americans. We assume our questions and assignments are clear and, in actuality, they may only be clear to us.

Most of the children involved in the southwest Colorado case study possessed a wealth of knowledge regarding the food, shelter, and tools of ancestral Pueblo people but they did not necessarily structure this information in the way that their teachers would prefer, or that I expected. When I originally asked students to construct a concept map of ancestral Pueblo life, I gave them the freedom to structure the information in the way that worked for them. In my own mind I was seeing time periods but nowhere in the instruction did I specifically ask students to organize their information chronologically. I simply assumed that my construction would be theirs. If I really wanted to examine their understanding of Pueblo cultural chronology, I should have also asked them to construct a time line, but that would have answered a different question; it would not have shown me how *they* structure their knowledge of Pueblo history. Through direct questions, I could see that the fifteen students who were interviewed knew that Pueblo lifestyle changed over time; an activity structured around a linear concept of time would have possibly shown the same results for the larger group.

As I interviewed students and asked them to explain some of the so-called misconceptions from their maps, I could almost hear them thinking, "If you wanted me to do it that way, why didn't you say so?" The point here is that I did not say so but somehow expected their work to look as if I had. It was an assumption that I had made but not recognized until I reflected on the experience. If I had asked each student to draw an elephant, would I have expected everyone to color his or her elephant gray and place it in a grassland setting? If they had drawn a brightly costumed circus elephant, would I have labeled their construction a misconception?

Misconceptions occur when individuals are confused regarding the way bits of information are linked together, or when they have inaccurate or incomplete information. Misconceptions regarding the Pueblo past certainly existed among the case study group. Ricky, for example, was trying to find a way to place evolution and early humans within his construction of the Pueblo past but did not understand how far apart in time these would have been. However, to assume that all mixes of time periods on these maps were due to misconceptions would itself be a misconception. They were only misconceptions when students, on questioning, could not organize the information sequentially. They were not misconceptions when students could move flexibly between a linear construction of the past and their own collages from which they drew meaning.

The constructions that we, as educators, possess regarding conceptual development in children may be so firmly fixed that we become blind to the ways children are actually using subject matter. It is important to ask ourselves if we have been explicit regarding the way we would like students to structure their responses, or if we have assumed that the structure was self-evident. It is also important to examine our own internal structure of the subject matter and to question how this perspective influences our understanding of what students are learning.

Assumptions regarding developmentally appropriate instruction also impose very rigid and limiting boundaries on what children are able to learn about the past. In curriculum development, knowledge of the most appropriate methods of instruction for a particular age/grade level is essential. The emphasis, however, should be on method and not content. A misread of developmental theory by many educators has resulted in watered-down and superficial educational content for elementary-aged students. An emphasis on only the concrete has drained much subject matter of the richness that can make it meaningful to children. Developmentally appropriate instructional activities for elementary school students need to reflect a consideration of methodological issues such as attention span, the importance of experience to learning, and the social needs of the learner. Instead, what often happens is the censorship of abstract concepts, leading to the development of instructional activities and materials that contain little substance. Students are presented with the same set of information over and over again; it is what prevents studies of Native American cultures from moving beyond corn, beans, and squash. It is also why multicultural studies are often reduced to learning about traditional foods and celebrations. Even if the instructional activities are experience based, little will be gained if students are not presented with information worth thinking about.

Again, using the case study as an example, teachers seldom used textbooks, and instructional methods in the classroom and at Crow Canyon seemed to be developmentally appropriate in nature. However, data gathered in the research project indicate that a discrepancy existed between the kinds of things children were learning and the kinds of things they were curious about. At the beginning of the unit of study, virtually every student could generate a long list of objects and activities associated with the Pueblo past but seemed to know little regarding patterns of change, the natural environment, or social structure. I believe it is reasonable to say that they were limited by the kinds of information they had been allowed to encounter and not by what they were capable of learning.

Admittedly, some of the questions posed by the students in the case study deal with issues that are difficult to explore when no written record exists, particularly information regarding ideology and the social world of past peoples. These aspects of culture are, however, of great interest to scholars who do develop theories and write about these issues. Educators may assume that these ideas are too esoteric for elementary-age students, but when children are posing some of the same questions as the scholars who develop the theories, I believe they are ready for more sophistication in their studies. A great deal of the curricula designed for environmental education has embraced this understanding. Many environmental science programs for the elementary grades are designed to move children beyond a dichotomous treatment of subject matter and into exploring the complexities surrounding important issues.

Children learn that preserving rainforests, stopping poachers, and saving endangered species are multifaceted problems. They become passionately involved in thinking about these issues and in trying to solve them. If fourth graders can understand the intricate web of an ecosystem, then it seems reasonable that they might also be able to comprehend, for example, the impact of increased population on social dynamics or on subsistence strategies. Assuming that students can only relate to a past that consists of a collection of nouns (corn, pottery, baskets, etc.) and a few simple verbs (hunt, gather, farm, etc.) places severe restrictions on learning. During high school, I took a basic French course but found it difficult to form any meaningful sentences or ideas from the small collection of nouns and verbs that were presented in the silly dialogs I was required to memorize. The same might be said for history or cultural studies that are equally grounded in the concrete.

Reflective practice is essential to effective instruction but it seems to be the aspect of education that is most easily omitted. This is in part due to the demands placed on educators across many different kinds of instructional settings. Time for reflection may seem like a luxury for educators who are already stretched thin by other expectations placed on them. There is, however, an even greater impediment to reflective practice and that is the body of myth that exists within the education profession. For consistency with my use of the term elsewhere in this book, I use myth here to refer to the beliefs of the profession that have become so engrained as to achieve a taken-for-granted status. What we believe regarding developmentally appropriate practice would fall into the realm of educational myth and we fail to question what the concept truly means. When beliefs become myth, their origins are no longer visible and we forget that they were once created. The way that developmentally appropriate practice is interpreted in contemporary educational circles may be light years removed from the way it was originally conceived. The impact this can have on history instruction is significant. When narratives of the past are drained of complexity, they soon become the hollow, lifeless stories that students will not listen to. It is essential that we continue to challenge our own perspectives and those of the educational profession if we are to create programs where learners can construct meaningful knowledge about the past.

Making History: Instructional Issues

Text and Context

Text is traditionally defined as words, writing, or printed matter. That objects or illustrations can also be considered texts, that they are open to interpretation, and that they may be read is a broader definition of the term. This expanded understanding of text is important to a number of disciplines, including sociocultural anthropology, archaeology, art, psychology, history, and folklore. Archaeologist Christopher Tilley states:

> Material culture is a framing and communicative medium involved in social practice. It can be used for transforming, storing or preserving social information. It also forms a symbolic medium for social practice, acting dialectically in relation to that practice. It can be regarded as a kind of text, a silent form of writing and discourse; quite literally, a channel of reified and objectified expression.
>
> Although material culture may be produced by individuals, it is always a social production. This is because it does not seem to be at all fruitful to pursue a view of the human subject as endowed with unique capacities and attributes, as the source of social relations, font of meaning, knowledge and actions. . . . In regarding material culture as socially produced, an emphasis is being placed on the constructedness of human meaning as a product of shared systems of signification. The individual does not so much construct material culture or language, but is rather constructed through them. [Tilly 1989]

A psychological perspective regarding the relationship between people and objects, offered by Mihaly Csikszentmihalyi, is that we objectify self through the things we make and possess. In his explanation of how objects represent us, he includes their role as symbols of power and status, as symbols of valued relationships, and as evidence that we have continuity through time. In a larger sense he says that the objects we choose to have around us stabilize our sense of who we are and reinforce our opinions of ourselves (Csikszentmihalyi 1993). As noted in chapter 2, poet Walt Whitman wrote about humans and the objects they surround themselves with as being engaged in more of a reciprocal relationship:

> There was a child went forth every day,
> And the first object he looked upon, that object he became,
> And that object became part of him for the day or a certain part of the day
> Or for many years or stretching cycles of years.
> [Walt Whitman 1959:138]

These three perspectives on objects as text, one from a poet, one from an archaeologist, and one from a psychologist, differ only slightly. Tilly places an emphasis on objects as signifiers of aspects of the social world to which an individual is a part of and on the importance of material culture to the construction of the individual. Csikszentmihalyi focuses on the way objects are an expression of self and, thus, de-emphasizes the role of society. Whitman's words seem to embody both perspectives.

I would have to agree with Whitman. Objects or artifacts are caught up in a web of meaning that includes the social and personal world of the object's creator as well as the world of each individual who examines it. The objects carry signification from both of those worlds and meaning is imposed in both directions.

I was interested in learning what type of artifacts the students involved in the case study had been particularly drawn to, so I included an item that was designed to elicit this type of information in the follow-up survey (see appendix 3). Item 10 asked students to identify the "coolest" artifact they encountered during their stay at the Crow Canyon Archaeological Center. Responses from sixty-nine of the children reflected choices similar to those made by students during the interviews. Approximately 59 percent of the students were attracted to some type of pottery, and another 17 percent indicated that they preferred projectile points and/or atlatls (an unidentified student from Norton's class drew a Ninja throwing star beside his picture of the atlatl—I am guessing that it was Albert). Following these choices, students selected the fire-making kit, structures (such as towers or kivas), and manos and metates as their favorites. I was surprised to see their overwhelming preference for pottery; during my observations, it seemed that children were more drawn to the atlatls and spears. They had certainly handled them more than any of the other objects they encountered. According to the children, they selected various pieces of pottery as their favorites because:

It is 700 years old.
It has cool paintings.
The Anasazi touched it.
It was touched and made by the Anasazi.
The designs are so creative.

The most common response by far had to do with designs on the pots. Exactly what meaning students found in these objects I cannot say, but the fact that so many of them made the same choice may indicate a shared significance that would be linked to the social world rather than just to the individual's private world of meaning. If attached meanings were just local and personal it seems that a more diverse selection of artifacts would be indicated.

Archaeologists stress the importance of artifact context to interpretation; an object is most meaningful when understood in relation to its exact spatial location and in relation to other objects that may be situated around it. Some of the students in this study expressed their preference for Yellow Jacket Pueblo over Mesa Verde, explaining that there were more artifacts on the ground at Yellow Jacket. Others spoke of the emptiness of the pithouse at Crow Canyon, saying that it did not look lived in. Objects take on meaning through context, through their situatedness. When objects are removed from the context in which they were used, the meaning changes, and when no context clues exist the object becomes even more situated in the context of self. Interpretation is an essential component of history education and of learning history. If students are expected to arrive at sound interpretations, they must be provided with contextual information.

Relevant But Not Relative

People use the past in many varied and creative ways to suit their own needs and their own feelings about their position in the world. . . . . If ideology is only partially consumed, and people create their own versions of the past, does this therefore mean that the content of museum displays is irrelevant? [Merriman 1991:131]

In the southwest Colorado case study, fourth-grade students who were studying the Pueblo past constructed at least two histories from the information that was presented to them. One of these histories was a reflection of the legitimized, linear conception of time that is taught in schools and is associated with a scholarly study of the past. The other was a synchronic construction that was comprised of meaningful objects, ideas, and events; it was a collage of the past. Students could usually produce a chronological story of the past when they were put to the test, so to speak. They could order events in time if specifically asked to do so. Where this instruction was not given, students selected the pieces of the past that they found most useful for constructing a personally meaningful narrative.

This brings us to the problem posed by Merriman: how do we teach people about the past in ways that engage them, without taking a relativist approach to history? The following discussion addresses this dilemma; it is not meant to be comprehensive but to revisit a few key points.

Experience has taught me that students are often the best experts regarding their own learning. Regardless of age, most students can identify what they like to study and how they like to learn. The follow-up survey for the case study asked students to identify, from a list of ten possibilities, the three ways they most liked to learn about the past. The results shown in table 7.1 indicate that the children who participated in the research project most like to study the past when it is contextualized—when they can examine the pieces of the past in relation to one another rather than in isolation.

The top three responses are methods that provide context for information about the past. Students overwhelmingly selected the living history option above all the others. This choice not only places objects and information within a specific context, it also provides students with the greatest number of ways to examine and process the information. Through contact with objects in their appropriate setting, students can touch, see, smell, hear, and, in some cases, taste the data. Museum visits—the second choice—provide powerful three-dimensional images and frequently place the images in a reproduced context such as a diorama or a reconstructed setting. Most museum exhibits are, however, more limited in sensory appeal than are the living history experiences. The third and fourth choices, videos and computers, provide powerful visual images and involve technologies that young people in particular, are highly drawn to.

Table 7.1.   Preferred Methods for Learning about the Past Reported by Case Study Participants

Instructional Method	Responses
1. Living History and Hands-on Experiences	46
2. Museum Visits	28
3. Video of the Way People Lived in the Past	25
4. Computers and Special Software	24
5. Artifact Analysis and Interpretation	16
6. Historic Fiction	15
7. Historic or Archaeological Site Visits	14
8. Board Games or Simulation	12
9. Storytelling	9
10. Informational Book	6

The only surprising outcome from the survey was the low ranking of story-telling, which came in next to last. If narrative is central to the way the children in the study were constructing the past, it seems that storytelling should be near the top of the list. What the term storytelling meant to these children is difficult to say. Formal storytelling programs for schoolchildren are often designed with only entertainment in mind and may be superficial in nature. Perhaps the students in the study associated storytelling with more whimsical tales and could not imagine how it could be used to teach something as serious as the human past. Another explanation, and one that I think is more likely, is that, for children, storytelling is usually about listening—not telling. Storytelling is a very different activity for the teller than for the listener. Story listening is a passive activity and one that is difficult for some children. Storytelling, on the other hand, is a dramatic perform-ance and the story that is told belongs to the teller. How children ranked storytelling on this questionnaire may be directly related to how they experience the act of storytelling.

The method for learning about the past that fell into last place was the in-formational book. The meaningful past constructed by children in this study was generally the narrative version that utilized images that were personally or socially significant. The informational book is the choice that is most void of narrative. It is also, ironically, the most common method for teaching history in schools. What these children have indicated, and what the case study suggests, is that we can better understand the past when evidence is provided that makes the past seem real, and when the individual is afforded the opportunity to participate in interpretation.

As I've said many times in this book, even the most stimulating instructional methods are irrelevant if the content is shallow or narrow and exclusive in focus. Through the case study interviews and surveys, I attempted to discover what his-torical content the students were most interested in learning about. I asked them where they would go if they had the opportunity to travel in time. A few students reported that they would visit the future and a few indicated that they would like to go all the way back to the Jurassic period. However, most of them said that they would like to visit the Four Corners area when the ancestral Pueblo people had been living there. Several students said they would like to visit Waterville during the days of pioneer settlement, and a few identified places and times that sounded more exotic, such as Europe during World War II. Overall, these fourth graders were interested in a past that was local and accessible to them. As one of the boys stated in our closing discussion, "This past seems real because we can see the ev-idence." The questions students posed regarding the Pueblo past showed that they most wanted to understand social dynamics and the way people dealt with life on a daily basis.

The kind of historical study that the students reported they were interested in corresponds fairly closely with the scope and sequence of history instruction in the United States. We generally teach local and state history in the lower grades, then move beyond these borders as children progress into middle and high school. So it seems that what we need to address in the elementary grades is how we teach that content and how we can help students learn more about those aspects of the local past that they are asking questions about. We need to expand on what counts as text in history classes and we need to provide students with evidence that they can evaluate and use in constructing their knowledge about the past.

Essential Points: A Review

In part I of this book, I attempted to describe the status of history/archaeology education in the United States, and identify what we do and do not know about learning history. Part II is a detailed account of a research project I conducted to better understand how students construct the past. In that section, I also provide a framework that shows how learners make meaning of the past. In this chapter, I have tried to synthesize some of the points brought forward in parts I and II and emphasize how these understandings are important to the practice of teaching the human past; I will close the chapter with a review of these essential points. I hope that this summary will prove useful for program development, as well as for program evaluation.

- Historical knowledge can be structured in at least two ways: narrative understanding and logical-scientific understanding. Narrative structure is used to convey essential meanings and may not adhere to a strict chronological/linear view of past events. This does not mean that narrative is an invalid approach to understanding past human events but that the meaningful sequence is not necessarily chronological. The way in which historical knowledge is constructed may vary cross-culturally.
- History should be viewed as all of the human past, not just the written past. To believe otherwise is to deny the legitimacy of the past of many groups of people.
- Knowledge of the past is constructed and learners enter into studies of the past with preconceptions. Discovering learner preconceptions is an important step in the development of effective and meaningful learning experiences.
- What educators believe they are teaching may not, in fact, be what students are learning. Thus, the ongoing examination of students' conceptual understandings is an important aspect of the instructional process. This may best be achieved through engaging students in dialog about their perceptions.

- We, as educators, have our own assumptions regarding the audiences we teach. These assumptions may be both personal and professional in nature. It is critical that we recognize our assumptions, understand how they shape instructional design, and examine how they may place constraints on what is learned.

- Meaningful learning requires active engagement in the construction of knowledge. People become engaged in studies of the past when they understand that history is made, when they are shown how it is made, and when they are provided opportunities to share in its construction.

- Multiple modes of instruction, particularly visual information, help students make meaning of the past. Therefore, it is important to interrogate instructional materials for their potential to inform as well as misinform. What is the possibility that the information may be misunderstood or erroneously interpreted?

- The context or setting in which instruction takes place is an important and powerful part of the instruction. For example, when artifacts are being used to teach about a past culture, the setting in which the learner encounters the artifacts will influence what is learned. In museums, this includes specific exhibits as well as the museum itself. The natural landscape can be a powerful context for teaching about the past. Connections can be made regarding the ways in which people across time have addressed basic needs in a particular setting and how they have used natural resources from that setting. Inferences can be made regarding the ways that various cultural groups have viewed the natural world based on their behaviors within it.

- Objects (artifacts, ancient structures, replicas, etc.) contribute to a learner's understanding of life in the past in a way that words alone cannot convey. This is particularly true for objects that can be held or used in some way. Authentic objects play a different role than replicas in the construction of knowledge about the past. Authentic or "real" objects are direct evidence of the past, whereas replicas are generally used to teach concepts about life in the past.

- If learners are to make meaning of the past, it must have relevance for them. This is one of the most important challenges for history and archaeology educators. Some common ways of establishing relevance include examination of the daily tasks of "ordinary people," research into personal and family histories, the study of one's community or cultural group, and studies of one's own gender or peer group in a particular historical era.

- Learners become more engaged in studies of the past when they are actively involved in constructing it. This requires a heavy emphasis on inquiry in the instructional process.

History as a Dialogic Practice: 8
Sharing Authority for Constructing the Past

Introduction

EDUCATIONAL RESEARCHERS ARE OFTEN ACCUSED of failing to show how their findings can be clearly translated into educational practice. Perhaps this is true for research in any discipline; those who conduct research and those who are practitioners are generally not one and the same. The purpose of this chapter is to address this challenge by providing examples that illustrate how the essential points summarized in chapter 7 can inform the development of educational programs in a variety of settings: a middle school classroom, an archaeological park/museum, and an informal education program.

I have chosen to limit my discussion of educational practice to the teaching of one particular topic to show more clearly how the research findings discussed in this book can be used across both formal and informal education programs. Specifically, I focus on the pre-Columbian[1] history of the Four Corners region. This includes the spread of human societies and the rise of diverse cultures, from dispersed bands of nomadic hunter-gatherers to large farming communities. There are two primary reasons for selecting this topic: first, it is the era of human history that is highlighted elsewhere in this book, and second, it directly addresses the National Standards for History:

The National Standards for U.S. History (Era I, Standard IA):
The student understands the patterns of change in indigenous societies in the Americas up to the Columbian voyages. [National Center for History in the Schools 1996:77]

In addition to the correlation with history standards, pre-Columbian history in the Four Corners region also deals with some of the major themes of the Curriculum Standards for Social Studies:

- Theme I: Culture
- Theme II: Time, Continuity, and Change
- Theme III: People, Places, and Environments [National Council for the Social Studies 1994]

Only one of the three settings discussed in this chapter—the middle school—is required to address national education standards. However, informal education programs should also consider what influences public education, because a large segment of their clientele is likely to come from this sector.

In terms of teaching about the past, there are advantages, as well as disadvantages, in both formal and informal education settings. The formal classroom may offer the greatest opportunity for in-depth study, depending on the structure of the school day and the freedom that teachers have in developing the curricula. It is also the most ideal setting to assess what is learned. Assuming that students are with a given teacher for a full year, or at least a semester, it is also the best situation for understanding the learner and adapting instruction to specific learning styles. The disadvantages of a formal school setting include the lack of access to authentic cultural materials or replicas, distance from the place in which the history is situated and, along with this, distance from the modern descendants of the people whose history is being studied.

History/archaeology education programs that take place in museums, parks, monuments, etc., have the obvious advantage of being able to bring visitors into direct contact with the material remains of past cultures. In many cases, they can also provide a sense of place—the authentic environment in which past peoples lived. Artifacts that are viewed in situ, or the remains of ancient structures that are still visible on the landscape, enhance the learning experience. Also, replicas that are located in authentic settings tend to have a more powerful effect on learning than those placed in an unrelated context. The primary disadvantage of teaching history in museums, parks, and other similar settings is the limited amount of contact that educators or interpreters have with visitors. In many cases, the only contact with visitors may be that which occurs through signage or other print materials. This is often due to inadequate funding. Where guided tours are conducted, they generally don't last longer than an hour or two. It is also difficult to conduct tours in a way that allows for dialog; they more often take the form of walking lectures with a limited amount of time for questions. Education in informal settings is also complicated by the lack of knowledge regarding who the visitors are, what they know, and what they are learning.

The multi-day education program, conducted in an informal setting, is probably the most unique of the approaches discussed in this chapter. There is considerable variation in such programs, depending on their primary mission and their structure for program delivery. For instance, some programs of this type are not located in one place, but travel to several different places related to the study of a particular cultural history. Scholars who are considered experts in their field usually accompany these traveling seminars and act as the primary instructors for them. Some institutions that conduct archaeological or historical research also provide on-site, multi-day education programs. These have a number of important advantages, including a more in-depth study of the topic than is possible in museums or parks; they are frequently situated in authentic settings; and they are often taught by people with a great deal of expertise in the particular subject area. The main disadvantage is that, although students are involved for an extended period of time, programs rarely last longer than a few days or weeks. Thus, there isn't a lot of time to learn about the learner—to design, modify, and adjust program content based on the students and their learning needs.

Because assessment of learning is critical to the improvement of history instruction in general, the discussion for each of the three settings includes assessment suggestions that are appropriate for the specific program. Chapter 9 provides greater detail about various assessment strategies and their value in understanding how learners construct the human past. Instruction in each of the three settings discussed in this chapter taps into, and takes advantage of, human curiosity as the ultimate tool to motivate learning. To this end, suggestions are given for evoking and utilizing learner questions in each of the three settings.

The process for developing the educational program in each of the settings is similar but the degree to which each element of the process is used varies between the formal and informal settings. The approach to curriculum development discussed and demonstrated in this chapter is in some ways my own but it would more appropriately be identified as a hybrid. I call it a hybrid, or blend, because I have drawn core elements from two important curriculum development models: *Understanding by Design*, which is the work of Grant Wiggins and Jay McTighe (1998), and Paideia Active Leaning, an educational reform model inspired by philosopher Mortimer Adler.

The strength of *Understanding by Design* is its big picture approach to curriculum development and the up-front attention given to assessment. It is particularly powerful in the way it continually causes the curriculum developer to focus on the significant understandings for a given unit of study.

Paideia well compliments *Understanding by Design* in that it is strong in the areas that are somewhat weak in *Understanding by Design*. While *Understanding by Design* provides a holistic structure for curriculum development, it does not focus heavily on instructional methods. *Paideia* fills this gap by offering very concrete guidance for the development of instructional activities that are active and intellectual in nature. *Paideia* is grounded in the belief that: "All genuine learning is active, not passive. . . . It is a process of discovery in which the student is the main agent, not the teacher" (Adler 1982).

In its earlier iteration, *Paideia* was criticized for being culturally narrow, meaning that Western knowledge was treated as legitimate knowledge, while non-Western forms of knowledge were basically ignored. However, under the leadership of Terry Roberts, director of the National Paideia Center, the Paideia view of what constitutes a classic work has greatly expanded to include far more than just the accepted Western classics. According to Roberts, a classic is provocative, rich in ideas, and worthy of multiple readings (Ruenzel 1997). Art and artifacts may qualify as a classic text using such a definition. In the Paidea model, instruction is a three-tier endeavor that includes seminars, intellectual coaching, and didactic instruction, with the emphasis on intellectual coaching. Didactic instruction is used to impart organized knowledge, coaching is for the development of intellectual skills, and seminars are designed to increase understanding of ideas and values. Seminars and intellectual coaching both stress the active engagement of the learner. These three types of instruction are wrapped into what Roberts refers to as the coached project:

> A Paideia Coached Project is a unit of study that leads to a student production or performance of real value to an audience outside the classroom. Coached Projects provide both teacher and students the opportunity to focus on the production of relevant academic work and to measure the quality of that work against authentic standards. Furthermore, Coached Projects contain all three elements of successful teaching and learning in a complementary whole: didactic instruction, coached skills practice, and seminar dialog. [National Paideia Center 2002]

Figure 8.1 illustrates the way in which I blend elements from these two models in the curriculum development process.

In this model, the parameters for the unit of study are things like eras, cultural groups, and geographic regions. Enduring understandings are the big ideas or essential concepts that learners should retain long after details are forgotten (Wiggins and McTigue 1998). Evidence of understanding would include performance tasks, unit projects or products, tests and quizzes, etc.

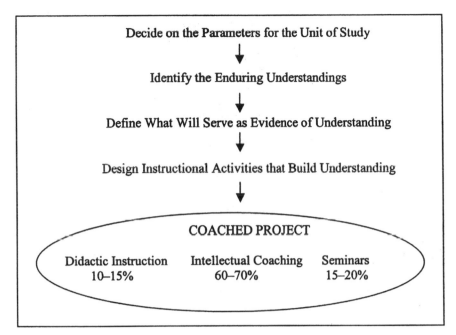

Figure 8.1.   Curriculum/Program Development Process

The reader should remember that the curriculum development process I am outlining here does not give an adequate description of either *Understanding by Design* or *Paideia*. I am simply touching on the basic tenets of each and showing how I integrate them into a process for developing curricula. Elements of each approach should be obvious in the following discussion of the three educational programs, particularly the program for the middle school classroom. Certain elements of the model do not fit as well with the informal programs. This is particularly true of the coached project; informal education programs generally do not have the participants or visitors involved for a long enough period of time to implement a coached project. However, some, like the Crow Canyon Archaeological Center, which is used as the final example in this chapter, provide an authentic educational experience by involving participants in an on-going research project.

The pre-Columbian history of the Four Corners region is immense and could be approached in a variety of ways. The examples given here are simply that—examples. They are designed to illustrate what history/archaeology education programs might look like when informed by the essential points brought forth in this book and when structured by the approach to curriculum development described above.

A Middle School Classroom

The geographic location of the classroom discussed in this section is outside of the Four Corners region. I have chosen a non-local setting to make the instructional activities described here more relevant to a larger number of educators, and also because much of the "long ago" is also far away—this is the reality that teachers face. They cannot step outside their schools and into the authentic contexts for the histories they teach. In choosing a non-local setting, I am challenging myself to address many of the same limitations that classroom teachers must consider when they design a unit of study.

I would also like to note two important assumptions that the following instructional plan is dependent on. The first is that students have had prior instruction regarding the concept of culture. In order to enter into any kind of abstract or analytical thinking regarding a specific culture, students need to have had an introduction to some of the foundational understandings. Included in this would be knowledge of some of the fundamental elements of culture (language, beliefs, etc.) and ways that culture influences the choices made by those who share the culture.

Enduring Understandings and Guiding Questions

There are three basic understandings for this unit of study:

1. Some of the cultural traditions practiced by the ancestral Pueblo peoples changed across time and others continued from generation to generation. Their descendants who live in the present-day Pueblo communities located in Arizona and New Mexico still maintain some of the ancient traditions.
2. The natural environment of the Four Corners includes multiple bio regions that were maximized by the ancestral Pueblo peoples for farming, hunting, gathering, and resource procurement.
3. Archaeologists interpret the past by using scientific methods to recover and analyze the material remains of a culture, and they also consult members of descendant communities to learn how they perceive/explain their own past.

In order to frame the unit in terms of intellectual inquiry, these understandings are reflected in guiding questions:

1. What were the lifestyles of the people who settled in the Four Corners prior to European contact? How did their lifestyles change across time? How did they remain the same?

2. What evidence is there to link the ancestral Pueblo peoples with the modern-day Pueblo peoples?
3. How did the ancestral Pueblo peoples meet their basic needs?
4. How did the environment influence the lifestyles of the ancestral Pueblo people? How did their lifestyles affect the environment?
5. How do archaeologists learn about those parts of the past for which there is no written record?

The activities that follow are designed to help students consider and develop understanding around these questions.

Assessing Prior Knowledge

Assessing prior knowledge is a critical step in the instructional process; it is impossible to discover what students are learning without establishing some type of baseline for comparison. It is also necessary to have information about students' naive conceptions and prior knowledge in order to understand how to adjust the curriculum to help students achieve targeted expectations.

Concept maps are highly useful for examining student thought before a unit of study. The maps can reflect what a student thinks and believes about a topic; they can also show how the student structures her or his knowledge. For example, the pre-Columbian history of the Four Corners could serve as the main topic around which students would develop concept maps. A more in-depth discussion of concept maps and the various ways in which they can be used is given in chapter 9.

Other useful forms of preassessment in a school setting include group interviews or surveys where students identify what they know and believe about the topic, self-assessments where students evaluate their current knowledge level about various aspects of the subject matter, and checklists where students are asked to agree or disagree with statements about the topic.

A simple way to assess the knowledge of a small group of students, or the entire class, is to create a chart that is completed by the students in a collaborative way. To assess prior knowledge regarding the ancient people of the Four Corners region, students would be asked to complete a chart indicating what they confidently know and believe, as well as those things that they find confusing (table 8.1).

Students should be instructed to think about changes and continuity over time regarding things like houses/shelter, environment, technology, settlement size, subsistence patterns, etc. Once constructed, this chart may be revisited throughout the unit as a kind of formative assessment; it could also be used as a part of the summative evaluation.

Table 8.1.   Student Preassessment: Ancient Peoples of the Four Corners

Knowledge	Beliefs	Things I Am Unsure Of
They were farmers.	They were great artists.	They moved away because
They grew corn, beans, and	They were happy.	of a long drought.
squash.	Their life was hard.	They were related to people
They lived in pithouses first,		in Mexico.
then in pueblos made of		They were small.
stone.		

Of all these preassessment strategies, the concept map is probably the most useful because of its open-ended nature, its power to show the depth of knowledge the students possess, and its potential for revealing the ways in which students are constructing knowledge.

The Unit Project

The final performance goal, or product, for this unit of study is a symposium that is modeled after those that take place at professional meetings for archaeologists. The audience for the symposium could be parents and other family members but it could also be the members of a local archaeological society, another class in the school, or even docents from a history museum.

The topic of the symposium is *Ancestral Pueblo History in the Four Corners Region*. In the symposium, students have the option of presenting their work through formal papers, posters, PowerPoint programs, or slide shows. These products might be the work of one individual or of small groups. Students should use the guiding questions to focus their work, but this does not mean that a particular presentation has to provide the comprehensive answer to a specific guiding question. For example, if a student were interested in the environmental question, a presentation that deals with one aspect of the problem, such as how environmental factors may have influenced the placement of ancient gardens, would be highly appropriate.

The classroom activities included in the unit are designed to build understanding related to the guiding questions and to prepare students with the knowledge, skills, concepts, and values that are needed for successful participation in the symposium.

Getting the Students Engaged in Learning: A Seminar

A critical step in designing any learning experience is providing students with the opportunity to become intrigued by the subject matter. Throughout this book, I have referred to problems with the way that history has traditionally been taught in school, particularly that it has often been perceived as boring. This is, to a large degree, a problem of motivation and of expecting students to share the motivations of the curriculum developers or their teachers. The introduction to any unit of study should be designed to help students find their own place of entry into the subject matter, to allow them to define for themselves a reason to learn more, to be curious. Such lessons need not be complex but they do need to be somewhat open ended. They should provoke questions in the minds of the learners, explore ideas and values, and promote understanding. Seminars are ideal for achieving this goal. The National Paideia Center defines a seminar as a collaborative, intellectual dialogue facilitated with open-ended questions about a text (National Paideia Center 2002). Central to a successful seminar is discourse between students rather than a volley of dialog between students and the teacher.

For an introductory seminar on pre-Columbian history in the Four Corners region, one might consider using the same stimuli that triggered the early European settlers and explorers' fascination with the area's ancient history—the remains of the ancient sandstone houses and villages. Images of these structures as they appeared at the time of homesteading in the late 1800s are preserved in historic photographs that were taken by well-known photographers like William Henry Jackson and early archaeologists like Gustaf Nordenskiold. Many such photographs are archived at Mesa Verde National Park, but the largest, most accessible collection may be that of the Denver Public Library's Western History and Genealogy Department. Over 100,000 historic photographs from their collection have been digitized and can be accessed through the Internet at photoswest.org. The photograph that serves as the text for the following seminar plan can be found at that web site (call number: Z-1303). It is a photograph of Mesa Verde's Cliff Palace and was taken by Thomas Michael McKee in 1900.

A formal seminar, as defined in the Paideia framework, includes four parts: the seminar text, questions, facilitation, and participation. The seminar plan given here presents only the first two parts, the text—in this case the historic photograph—and the questions. The skillful facilitation of seminars is an ability that is acquired through training and practice; guidance for doing so is beyond the scope of this discussion. The National Paideia Center in Chapel Hill, North Carolina, provides both training and materials for conducting formal seminars.

SEMINAR PLAN FOR CLIFF PALACE HISTORIC PHOTOGRAPH

Pre-Seminar   Provide students with some background information regarding the discovery of Cliff Palace. This should include the fact that the Utes were the first people who came into the area after the Pueblo people moved away in the late 1200s and, thus, they would be the true discoverers of Cliff Palace, as well as the other Pueblo ruins on Mesa Verde. Navajos were, according to archaeologists, the next people to come into the area. Due to traditional spiritual beliefs, neither the Utes nor the Navajos disturbed the ruins; they knew about them but did not explore them. Spanish explorers passed through the area and made note of some ancient Pueblos but none were on Mesa Verde. It was not until the late 1800s that Cliff Palace and the other ancient Pueblo villages were brought to the attention of the world. A ranching family from Mancos, Colorado—the Wetherills—is credited with making these sites visible outside the Four Corners. The Wetherills knew about, and had seen, many ancient ruins in the area but they became particularly interested in the well-preserved alcove sites that they encountered on Mesa Verde when they began grazing cattle there in the 1880s.

Opening Questions
- What name would you give this place? Why? (If students already know that it is called Cliff Palace, ask them to suspend that knowledge and create a new name.)
- Do you find this place intriguing? Why or why not?

Core Questions
- If you were with Richard Wetherill when he first saw this place in the late 1800s, what questions would have come to your mind?
- Which questions do you think have been satisfactorily answered? Which questions might endure today?
- What assumptions or misconceptions do you think the early European settlers might have had about the ruins and their creators?

Closing Questions
- If you could be anywhere in this picture, where would you choose to be? Why?

POST-SEMINAR After students have participated in the seminar and heard the ideas and questions of others, have them each make a list of the five questions that she or he would most like to have answered about this ancient village. Then have them list the kinds of evidence that they might look for if they were archaeologists trying to answer these questions.

Constructing the Past through Archaeology: An Inquiry Lesson for Learning Cultural Chronology

As I have pointed out elsewhere in this book, it cannot be assumed that people outside the scholarly world of historians and archaeologists have a linear understanding of the past. While I believe that a linear view should not be considered the only valid perspective, the chronological ordering of information is still necessary for understanding cultural continuity and change, interpreting historical and archaeological data, making logical inferences about the past, and gaining insight into life in the present. History does matter, and it is important to present events and eras in a structure that fosters historical thinking; this requires a sequential frame that provides temporal context. In earlier chapters, I have talked about the distaste that many people seem to have for the presentation of historical information as a string of names and dates. The teaching suggestion that follows is, I hope, more intellectually stimulating than the memorization of facts on a time line. It engages students in the process of inquiry, teaches the cultural chronology of the Four Corners before European contact, and reveals methods archaeologists use to construct the past.

The Native peoples who lived in the Americas before European contact did not have a written language, thus, what is known about them is learned through archaeological and ethnohistorical research. Rather than tell students about archaeologists' interpretations of this "time before history," assemblages of replica artifacts can be used as the evidence from which students gather their own information. An assemblage is a group of artifacts recurring together at a particular time and place. They are assumed to be reflections of the activities in which a group of people commonly participated. Admittedly, this approach involves a great deal of preparation, but the learning that can result is considerable. Not only do students have an opportunity to understand how history is made from the unwritten record, they are able to construct their own knowledge. As I have stressed throughout this book, learning of this type is not borrowed, it is owned.

Museums may have teaching kits with artifact assemblages that educators can borrow for use in their classrooms. Anthropology departments at colleges and universities may also have unprovenienced artifacts that they loan for educational purposes. Artifact assemblages can also be created using illustrations if the actual objects or replicas are not available. An excellent example of this is the illustrated assemblage developed for *Intrigue of the Past: North Carolina's First Peoples* (Price, Samford, and Steponaitis 2001). Don't collect artifacts in order to create teaching kits. Any activity that encourages the removal of artifacts from archaeological sites contributes to the destruction of those sites and the information they hold.

Using artifacts or their replicas for educational purposes is not new; however, these are probably used most often to teach about a particular time period rather than cultural continuity and change over a broad time span. The Crow Canyon Archaeological Center has developed two versions of an activity that utilizes artifact replicas for teaching about thousands of years of cultural history in the Four Corners. The version for younger students is titled *Windows into the Past*; the one for older students and adults is called *Inquiry into the Past*. *Windows into the Past* consolidates some of the archaeologically defined time periods in order to keep the information at a manageable level for younger students. Both of these activities were inspired by an activity called *Cultural History Mystery* that was created at the Center for American Archeology in Kampsville, Illinois. Following is a brief description of *Windows into the Past*; more specific directions for producing the artifact kits and teaching the activity can be found in *Windows into the Past: Crow Canyon Archaeological Center's Guide for Teachers* (Davis and Connolly 2000).

Artifact assemblages for three time periods are used in this version of *Windows into the Past* to give students a basic understanding of human occupation in the Four Corners region before A.D. 1500: Archaic (6500–1000 B.C.), Early Farmers (Basketmaker and Pueblo I, 1000 B.C. to A.D. 900), and Pueblo Farmers (Pueblo II and Pueblo III, A.D. 900–1300). After the ancient Pueblo Indians left the Four Corners area around A.D. 1300, Ute and Navajo people moved into the region. However, archaeologists who conduct research in the Four Corners believe that there was no significant population of these peoples until after A.D. 1500 (Lipe, Varien, and Wilshusen 1999:366). Thus, I am not including assemblages for these groups in the description of this activity. I have also not included a Paleo-Indian assemblage because, although there is evidence of people having moved through the region in the late Paleo period, it is scant and a replica assemblage for that time period would be somewhat contrived.

Each artifact assemblage should give evidence of the kinds of shelters being used by the people of that time period as well as their methods of subsistence and the kinds of technology that they relied on. Table 8.2 provides information regarding the contents of each assemblage. There are obviously many more or different items that could be included. Background research will help determine the essential items for inclusion in an artifact assemblage that is meant to reflect the behavior of a group of people living in a particular place in time.

Assuming that preconceptions have already been identified through the methods given previously, or via other strategies, this activity would begin with a clarification of terms such as: archaeology, anthropology, culture, artifact, ancestral Pueblo, and Anasazi. Some of these terms are obviously less complex than are others. Culture is a particularly difficult concept to grasp and even more difficult to convey to students. A few leading questions are useful for clarification. For example, students could be asked to think about the elements of culture that they can see and those that they cannot see. This line of questioning would also help students identify some basic assumptions within the discipline of archaeology, as well as some of its limitations for understanding past human cultures.

Following the discussion of terms, students should be given information regarding the goal of the lesson—to learn about cultural continuity and change through time in the Four Corners region. Using some common modern artifacts (such as a pencil, a coin, a soft drink can, and a backpack) the teacher should demonstrate how to observe and classify data. Students should be given the fol-

Table 8.2.   Contents of Artifact Assemblages

Time Period	Assemblages
Archaic	Atlatl, projectile point, spear, stone flakes, biscuit mano, fire-making tools, woven sandal, willow twig figure (deer), containers of seeds (salt bush, Indian rice grass, piñon pine, others), illustrations showing game animals, brush shelter, other items that cannot be represented by objects. Antlers or bones of animals could also be used to indicate what was being hunted.
Early Farmers	Small corncob, pinto beans, gourd, native wild plant seeds or plant materials, yucca fiber. Replicas of sifting basket and coil basket, bone awl, bone needle, fire-making tools, digging stick, crude stone axe, loaf-shaped mano, projectile points (both spear and arrow), stone flakes, bow, small clay figurine, cloud-blower pipe, pottery sherds or vessels appropriate for the time periods, chunks of burned adobe, illustrations (showing game animals, site maps, room block, more pottery).
Pueblo Farmers	Small corncob, blue cornmeal, pinto beans, gourd pottery scraper, wild plant material and seeds, yucca brush, raw cotton, coil basket, turkey eggshell. Replicas of a bone awl, bone scraper, bone chisel, bone die or gaming piece, projectile point (arrow only), stone flakes, drill, pecking stone, slab mano, pottery sherds and/or vessels appropriate for the time period, polishing stone, shell and turquoise beads, arrow, illustrations of game animals, site maps, PII great house, and cliff dwelling.

lowing categories for classifying the modern artifacts: tools, containers, subsistence (how people get their food or make a living), shelter, and other. Some of these may seem a bit ambiguous to students: is a backpack a tool or a container? Through discussion, the teacher can help develop criteria for making such decisions.

In this activity, it is also important that students understand the difference between an observation and an inference. For example, in an activity where students examine modern artifacts in an unidentified backpack, they sometimes interpret the presence of a crushed Coca-Cola can as evidence that the individual who owns the pack likes Coca-Cola. This would be an inference, not an observation. When moving from the observation to the inference stage, it is important to have students examine their conclusions to see if alternative explanations could exist— perhaps the individual with the crushed Coca-Cola can picks ups trash when he or she is hiking.

After moving through the example, students should be given a record sheet for classifying data in the assemblages (table 8.3). After they have recorded information for all three assemblages, they could try to place them in a sequence from the oldest time period to the most recent. Realistically, there is no reason that students should be able to successfully do this given the assemblages described in table 8.2.

Archaeologists in the Southwest generally depend on dates derived from the tree rings of construction timbers to establish chronologies. However, by asking students to place assemblages in the appropriate chronological sequence, two other goals can be achieved: (1) it provides a way to reveal naive conceptions that students may have regarding progress; and (2) it stimulates the students' desire to learn the correct sequence.

The wrap-up lecture and discussion should be structured according to the chronological sequence, and should draw on critical thinking skills and the use of evidence to support claims. Questions regarding specific artifacts can also be addressed during this discussion. The goal is to have students share inferences regarding each of the time periods and to relate these inferences to observations made about particular artifacts.

Stereotypes regarding Native Americans, life in the past, gender roles, etc., may surface during the wrap-up discussion. Having students confront their naive ideas and misconceptions can be an important outcome of this lesson. There are a number of ways to approach this, but the most effective are those methods that allow students to discover the errors in their thinking. Simply telling students that Pueblo people did not live in teepees will probably not change deeply embedded beliefs. Allowing them to discover this from evidence, such as drawings and photographs, will prove more successful. Moving students through conceptual change requires that they be dissatisfied with their existing views; visual messages are generally more powerful than verbal for accomplishing this.

A misconception that has been perpetuated for many decades is that the ancient Puebloan people (Anasazi) simply vanished. Changing this perception should be an additional focus of the closing discussion. Using maps of New Mexico and Arizona, as well as photographs showing modern Pueblos and contemporary Pueblo people, should cause students to recognize that, even though they no longer have villages in the Mesa Verde region, Pueblo communities and cultures are very much alive on the Hopi mesas in Arizona, and in the pueblos of Zuni, Acoma, and the Rio Grande River valley of New Mexico. A contemporary arti-

Table 8.3. Matrix for Classifying Assemblage Data

Assemblage	Subsistence	Shelter/Type of Settlement	Container	Tools	Other
A					
B					
C					

fact kit could be constructed to help make this point. At the end of the wrap-up, students should be able to identify aspects of Pueblo culture that have changed over time, as well as the traditions that have endured.

Illustrated time lines are highly appropriate for assessing student understanding of cultural chronology. These can be constructed cooperatively in small groups or individually. Rubrics should be developed for evaluating student work on the time lines.

Establishing a Sense of Place: Guided Independent Study

The environment informs and helps shape many different aspects of a culture, just as a cultural group's perspective regarding the natural world is reflected through their treatment of the environment. In a study of culture, people and place are inseparable. However, it can be difficult to convey the look and smell of a pinyon-juniper forest or a red sandstone canyon to students who have never experienced them firsthand. Students who, for example, are surrounded by deciduous forest, or reside in an urban canyon of concrete and glass, cannot fully understand or appreciate the character of areas like the Four Corners just by reading about them. The texture and color of a region are difficult to convey through textbook style description. Facts regarding climate, vegetation, geology, etc., are critical pieces of environmental information, but these remain sterile and remote when students cannot see how these parts are integrated to form the landscape, or how cultural groups form spiritual, emotional, and personal bonds with the landscape.

The questions that students' pose in the seminar previously described would almost certainly connect in some way to the natural environment of the Mesa Verde region. For example, if students are curious to learn why all the people left the area in the late 1200s, they will automatically be drawn into learning more about the environment. Even simple questions like "How did they build their houses?" or "Why did they choose to live on Mesa Verde?" require delving into information about natural resources and climate.

Multiple sources of information should be made available to students to help them build a more genuine understanding of the land known in modern times as the Four Corners. Such resources are not difficult to locate. The American Southwest has, for decades, been the subject of artists working in a variety of genres, from poetry and prose, to painting and photography. Supplementing research reports and other types of factual information with rich examples of artistic expression can enhance the students' understanding of the landscape and how people have related to it. As one of the most photographed areas in North America, it is not difficult to provide students with exquisite images of the varied landscapes that fall within the region. From William Henry Jackson, to Ansel Adams and Laura Gilpin, to Eliot Porter and David Muench, the American Southwest has been recorded in ways that not only document specific places in time, but that also reflect something of its character and spirit. Photographers have been drawn to the vastness of the sky and the quality of the light that are as much a part of the landscape as the red rocks and sagebrush. Countless painters have also found themselves captivated by these same qualities. When Georgia O'Keefe discovered the region, she spent the next fifty years trying to capture it on canvas. Writers as diverse as Willa Cather, Edward Abby, Terry Tempest Williams, and Leslie Marmon Silko have used words to depict the landscape and the human connection in a more literary or poetic way than can be conveyed in a geography book or field guide.

Although not found in a library or on the Internet, the colors and textures, the aromas and tastes of a place can also express volumes. As human beings, we experience our environment with five senses and in school we generally expect students to construct their knowledge using only one or two. Since, in the example constructed for this chapter, students cannot readily gain firsthand experience with the natural environment they are studying, the inclusion of specimens from the prevailing natural elements of the Four Corners—piñon, juniper, sage, and sandstone—can provide them with information about the region that they will not be able to gain in any other way.

Because knowledge of the environment is critical to understanding human history in the Four Corners, it is important to provide students with a way to show how they are synthesizing this kind of information. Students can provide evidence of their understanding in a number of ways, from displays of scientific data, to presentations of artistic expression. Illustrations showing the eco zones found at changing elevations in the region, charts or graphs reflecting various characteristics of the environment, landscape paintings, poems, essays, etc., are all ways that students can reflect on and demonstrate what they know and believe about the region's natural environment. The teacher's role in this process is to facilitate or coach independent study.

Formative Assessment

A great deal of information can be gained in the lessons described thus far. At this point it would be good to return to the preassessment chart that was constructed and have students add to and revise their earlier ideas. Keeping track of these changes can be a valuable way to conduct a formative assessment of student learning and the contributions made by different types of instruction.

Another valuable way to assess what students are understanding is to guide them in an examination of archaeological ways of knowing. Students should be asked to identify some of the assumptions that archaeology rests on and to consider how these assumptions affect the work that archaeologists do, as well as the conclusions that they reach. The purpose of this is not to undermine archaeological research in the eyes of the students but to have them recognize that, as with other ways of knowing the past, archaeology has strengths and weaknesses.

Through such activities, students become stronger critical thinkers and better prepared to evaluate evidence. Following is a discussion of how students could learn about the views that modern Pueblo people have of their ancient history. As students move through this portion of their studies, they should be asked to continue their consideration of archaeological ways of understanding the past and think about how traditional knowledge and archaeology can compliment, as well as contradict, each other. Students should be encouraged to examine and clarify their own opinions on the role that each of these approaches plays in expanding our knowledge of the past.

Pueblo Perspectives: Guided Independent Study

It would be a mistake to develop a unit of study on ancient Pueblo history that does not include the perspectives of modern Pueblo people. The methods of archaeological and historical research are grounded in scientific ways of understanding and explaining phenomena. That these are not the only approaches available for learning about the past is an important lesson in and of itself. Oral traditions can be particularly important for revealing aspects of history that may not be reflected in the archaeological record, as well as for looking at those that are not easily understood through the examination of material remains. Ideas about the nature of knowledge, fundamental assumptions regarding why the past is important, and even issues of time and space are all significant ways that archaeological and historical approaches differ from oral tradition.

> For some Native Americans, the past is a way to know the present, and, as such, something that happened centuries ago can have as much relevance to present-day issues as an event that happened last year. The length of time separating these events is not as important as the relevance of these events to present-day identity and life. [Anyon et al. 1997:82–83]

Students should have a chance to become familiar with the idea that the past may be used differently across cultures. Realizing this can help them consider multiple perspectives on the past without becoming overly frustrated by conflicting accounts.

Although not plentiful, accounts of ancient Pueblo Indian history that are based on oral tradition are available. Joe Sando's *Pueblo Nations: Eight Centuries of*

Pueblo Indian History (1998) includes a discussion of traditional Pueblo history that is a synthesis from several different Pueblo language groups. *The Pueblo* by Alfonso Ortiz (1994) of San Juan Pueblo also provides an account of Pueblo beginnings.

In conducting a search for traditional Pueblo accounts of the past, whether a library search or via the Internet, it is useful to search by the name of specific Pueblos, as well as by the generic classification. Several volumes of traditional Hopi stories have been written by Hopi people, or in collaboration with other writers. *Truth of a Hopi* by Edmund Nequatewa (1967) is a collection of origin stories and histories of Hopi clans. Leslie Marmon Silko (1993) has written extensively about the importance of oral tradition and stories at Laguna Pueblo.

Another approach to learning about Pueblo oral tradition is through ethnographic and ethno historical accounts that were recorded by anthropologists and sociologists in the early part of the twentieth century. Anthropologist Elsie Clews Parsons spent twenty-five years conducting ethnographic fieldwork in the Pueblos of the Southwest. Pioneer ethnologist Frank Hamilton Cushing lived at Zuni Pueblo in the nineteenth century and wrote extensively about Zuni oral tradition and beliefs. The problem, of course, is that these are not actually the perspectives of Pueblo people but, rather, secondhand accounts of their traditional stories. In addition, even though people like Parsons and Cushing spent a great deal of time in Pueblo communities, they were still outsiders and could only write about what they were permitted to see and hear.

For this unit of study, selected readings from the books previously mentioned, as well as from other personal accounts of Pueblo history and tradition, such as *My Life in San Juan Pueblo: Stories of Esther Martinez* (Jacobs et al. 2004), can be assigned to give students information from Pueblo perspectives.

Enriching Activities

Relevant field trips to archaeological or historic sites, museums, etc., as well as presentations by Pueblo peoples and archaeologists are also important ways to extend understanding. Bringing students into direct contact with ancestral Pueblo artifacts from the Four Corners can help them make a personal connection with the past and, as one student in the Colorado case study said, "This past seems real because you can see evidence of it." Although not as effective as seeing pottery sherds at the site of an ancient village, artifacts that are presented in museum exhibits can still provide students with a direct link to people in the past. Objects that were created by individuals from the era and/or cultural group being studied provide a kind of proof that transcends the years that separate the present from the past.

American youth who don't live near a large population of Native American people often think of Native people as belonging only to the past. For this reason, it is important to link studies of the Native American past with contemporary Native peoples and their communities. The most effective way to do this is, where possible, to take students into those communities. In conducting field trips of this nature, it is important to carefully prepare students so that they understand how to behave appropriately. They should know how to show respect for the people they will encounter on a reservation and for their privacy. They should receive guidance in knowing how to view things they see that may stand in stark contrast to their own community, or even seeming contradictions within the reservation itself. Field trips are enhanced by arranging in advance to have an individual from the host community accompany the students and help them understand the things they see and hear. These same guidelines apply equally to any community visit that is related to the study of culture and history. Where visits to Native American communities are not possible, classroom visits by Native people are also beneficial, as are well-constructed films and videos.

Images, whether real or virtual, are necessary for breaking down stereotypes and moving students through conceptual change. Sometimes a simple photograph can teach a powerful lesson. I distinctly remember one of my former students staring at a magazine photograph of a Native American boy who was preparing to dance in a powwow. He was dressed in full regalia except for his Nike sneakers. Starring at the photograph, the student insisted that, "This is not right." When I asked her to explain why, she said it was because the boy was supposed to wear moccasins. I don't think the little girl had ever been to a powwow so she had no knowledge of what would be considered appropriate attire, nor did she know that powwows are contemporary multicultural events through which new ways of dancing and dressing are constantly evolving. She had a vision of what she believed was the way that Indian people should dress and it was difficult for her to get her head around the notion that the boy could be Indian and still wear something that is practically a trademark of American pop culture. The photograph and our related conversation caused her to confront her misconceptions, which is an essential step toward changing them.

Assessing Learning

As an end-of-unit assessment, students should be evaluated on their contribution to the symposium. Students could also be asked to make final changes and additions to the preassessment documents they constructed, including the concept maps and the list of knowledge and beliefs regarding the history of Pueblo Indian people.

Museums and Archaeological Parks

Museums and archaeological parks in the Four Corners are not necessarily independent of one another. Archaeological parks often have their own museum or are associated with a nearby museum where artifacts from the park are curated. These informal settings are rich with material for teaching about the human past. They possess what, according to Rosenzweig and Thelen (1998), people most want from the past—the evidence. It is through cultural material that the realness of the past can be conveyed and from which stories about human life in the past can be constructed without the mediation of others.

Archaeological parks and museums have garnered much criticism for the distance they often create between artifacts and the people who come to see them. This is not a physical distance as much as a psychological one. Glass cases that are void of anything other than the artifacts themselves perpetuate the perception that artifacts should be viewed as treasures in and of themselves, rather than information about people and how they lived. To be fair, this approach probably does satisfy some museum visitors who already possess a high level of knowledge related to the objects. For example, potters might view an exquisite Mesa Verde black on white vessel with an eye for the quality of its form, its highly polished surface, and its carefully executed decoration. However, many other museum visitors who don't have this same level of knowledge may be more interested in what the vessel was used for, where it came from, or who the potter was. The last question is probably not answerable but, given enough information, the museum visitor can begin to form an image. This image is perhaps female, maybe a woman in the prime of her life who has mastered a craft and has the skill to produce the image of perfection that she sees with her mind's eye. The visitor with little background knowledge will have a more difficult time putting this image together. He or she might not be able to visualize the woman digging the clay, gathering the bee weed for her paint, or applying it with a few fine strands of yucca fiber.

Exhibits that supply contextual clues can help museum visitors construct a narrative of the past that is more human and less clinical than the barren glass case. Context is significant to learning in many different fields. Whether it is a young reader grappling with unfamiliar words, a detective trying to identify the events that occurred at the scene of a crime, or an archaeologist attempting to discern past human behavior, the making of meaning is highly dependent on contextual information.

Unlike the middle school example, which was located outside the Four Corners region, I have chosen to place the museum example within the region. The primary reason for doing this is to illustrate how a museum can take advantage of a variety of resources to build context for the cultural materials that will be used in an exhibit or educational program. Two assumptions come with this discussion. First is the assumption that the museum possesses an adequate collection of ancient Pueblo Indian artifacts from a specific context in the Four Corners region. Second is the assumption that the archaeological site associated with the artifacts is located near the museum.

The foremost educational goal of this program is that of engaging visitors in learning about Pueblo cultural history during the thirteenth century, a time of dramatic social change, and the period just preceding the final migrations out of the region. For reasons that are still unclear, settlement patterns experienced a radical shift during this time, from smaller, dispersed villages to large community centers that were generally located around the heads of canyons. Rather than draw from all, or even a few of these communities, the educational program discussed here provides an in-depth look at one of these large villages. In featuring one place, I hope to show how visitors could be involved in thinking about what it would take to build the village, as well as to manage and maintain it. The smaller scale of one village would, I believe, help visitors recognize more clearly the large-scale factors that might have influenced the social, cultural, and economic decisions that the people of the region made during the thirteenth century.

Neither the archaeological site nor the museum that I use in this example is a real place but, for the sake of discussion, I have chosen to give this imaginary facility a name; I refer to it as the Warm Springs Pueblo and Museum. There are, however, a number of facilities in the Four Corners that fit this pattern of archaeological sites paired with museums. Among these are the Anasazi Heritage Center in Dolores, Colorado, Edge of the Cedars in Blanding, Utah, and Aztec National Monument in Farmington, New Mexico. However, none of these institutions mentioned have, to my knowledge, the kind of educational program or exhibit that is described here, nor do any others that are located in the Four Corners. This is not meant as a criticism of any of these institutions; I point it out simply to clarify why I have chosen to place this example within a fictional setting.

Enduring Understandings

1. Some of the larger thirteenth-century villages had sizable populations, probably several hundred.

2. The complete migration out of the region by the end of the thirteenth century is still not well understood, but contemporary theories see this issue as being complex in nature and including a number of interrelated factors.

3. Villages the size of Warm Springs Pueblo would require cooperation on a number of different levels, including how the people of the pueblo

organized their village spatially, how they organized work for the completion of large projects, how they shared resources, and how decisions were made.

4. Archaeologists study social organization by looking at settlement patterns; this includes examining the scale and nature of individual sites and the relationship between sites.

Four questions developed from these understandings guide program and exhibit development:

1. What were ancestral Pueblo settlements like in the thirteenth century and how many people generally lived in a settlement?
2. What factors may have contributed to the complete migration of ancestral Pueblo people out of the area by A.D. 1300?
3. How did the people of Warm Springs Pueblo organize their village, make decisions, and accomplish their work?
4. What was the relationship between Warm Springs Pueblo and the other settlements around it?

The *Paideia* model is not as good a fit for the museum setting as it is for the middle school classroom. While it could work well for designing school group activities for the museum, its reliance on group discourse and extended projects make it less versatile when planning for a variety of group types as well as for individuals.

Visitor Studies and Preconceptions

In the previous example for a middle school setting, the examination of preconceptions was treated as one of the first activities within the unit of study. In the museum example, I am treating it as something that happens prior to the creation of exhibits or the development of educational curricula and materials. As I pointed out at the beginning of this chapter, each of the three settings discussed has a different set of advantages and disadvantages. Time for direct contact with the learner is generally shorter in the museum than in the other two settings and there is less potential for modifying the experience once the learner has already entered into it. Education in museums also depends more on independent, self-guided activities than does instruction in a classroom setting. Thus, information regarding preconceptions should be gained before the development of exhibits and programs in order to inform and help shape the educational experiences.

Museums and archaeological parks often have their own mythology regarding what visitors do and do not know. I refer to this as mythology because these stories of visitor knowledge, or the lack of it, have been passed among staff for so long that no one is sure of their origin. In many cases, the mythology is not grounded in visitor studies but in informal observations of what might be called, for lack of a better term, extreme visitor ignorance. To illustrate, at one archaeological park that I am choosing not to identify, some members of the interpretive staff share stories of the "stupidest questions" asked by visitors. For example: "At what elevation do deer become elk?" and "How many unidentified archaeological sites are in the park?" These questions are admittedly humorous and provide levity for those who have to conduct so many tours per day that visitors must seem like a sea of faces. Unfortunately, the collecting and telling of such questions can also reflect and encourage a lack of respect for visitors. It also prohibits further investigation to discover their preconceptions or to better understand how programs and exhibits can be improved. Visitor studies are essential for developing a better understanding of how museums and parks can meet the needs of their patrons and become more effective educators. If questions such as those previously mentioned represented the most commonly asked questions, then they might deserve the amount of attention they receive.

Visitor studies are complicated because they involve trying to understand the interests of multiple audiences. Considering that many museums and archaeological parks are inadequately funded, it also involves setting priorities regarding which of these groups should receive the most attention. Unfortunately, research always comes at a price and the lack of funds can end visitor studies before they have even begun. This seems to be a highly inefficient way to make decisions. At best, it's a trial-and-error approach; at worst, it says that visitors are not really very important to the museum. If this is true, that visitor perspectives are not really a priority, one is left with the question regarding the purpose of museums. If visitors are not a concern in the decision-making process in museums and archaeological parks, then we have to ask who or what *is* central to the decisions that are made. If education is truly embraced in the institutional mission, then visitor studies are a necessity. This is not only true for learning about preconceptions but also for gaining insight into an array of critical issues including demographics, interests, and questions visitors might have that are related to the content or topics that are the focus of programs and exhibits.

Another difficulty with visitor studies is that they are intrusive; they require the participation of visitors. Visitors, with the exception of school groups, are likely to be using their leisure time for the museum visit. Expecting them to respond to questions or permit an observer to "shadow" them on their tour may seem like a huge imposition—it is. Thus, it's important to establish some form of reciprocity that appropriately compensates visitors for their participation.

For the museum program in this example, visitor studies should focus on the preconceptions that members of the targeted group have in relation to the enduring understandings, as well as identify their interests related to the topic. Given that the program in this example is designed for general interest, a careful review of visitor demographics would need to be done to determine how to select a sample population for the study of preconceptions. This is important because museum visitation can have a very seasonal quality. For example, some museums tend to have more school groups in the spring and fall, families in the summer, and senior citizens in the winter. In such a setting, a study that is designed to include a random sample of visitors over a short period of time will not describe the whole population, regardless of how large the sample is.

A number of methods would be useful for gaining insight into what visitors of the Warm Springs Pueblo and Museum know or would like to learn about life in a thirteenth-century Pueblo village. All of these methods would be classified as front-end evaluations because they happen before the creation of exhibits or designing educational activities. They gather information to inform and help shape the educational program. Some of the methods used in front-end evaluations include focus group interviews, observations, questionnaires, and individual interviews. These could be designed to get at visitors' knowledge and interests in relation to some of the broader concepts identified in the enduring understandings.

Carefully designed interview guides and questionnaires could help uncover preconceptions that members of various groups have concerning these topics. Other ways of getting at this kind of information, as well as identifying the questions and interests of visitors, would include using some of the available materials or data to stimulate discussion and inquiry. For example, an artist's interpretation of what Warm Springs Pueblo might have looked like when it was occupied could be used in a focus group discussion with schoolchildren.

The Warm Springs Pueblo Education Project

Because the education project described here is invented solely for the purpose of illustrating some of the concepts brought forth in this book, it is not shaped by budgetary constraints. And, although some aspects of the project might be considered costly, they are not out of the realm of possibility for museums. This is evidenced by the fact that a number of the strategies included in the design of this project are already used in some museums outside the Four Corners.

The Warm Springs project is designed to effectively integrate exhibits, dioramas, computer interactives, guidebooks, and an actual tour of the archaeological site. The computer interactives draw from an electronic database that includes a wide variety of field and laboratory data from the archaeological research conducted at Warm Springs. The structure of the Warm Springs project is, in many ways, more like that of web-based educational activities or multimedia programs than a traditional museum environment. Studies of the way that learners navigate through multimedia environments recognize that there is great variation in the paths chosen. In other words, there doesn't seem to be one best way to enter into these electronic educational environments. Instead, students may use the programs in pursuit of multiple learning goals; they are treated as places to explore. This type of self-directed learning is rich with information that can be used to help shape actual learning environments of a constructivist nature. Following is a description of the various exhibits and educational tools for teaching about the Warm Springs Pueblo.

WARM SPRINGS PUEBLO: THE BIG PICTURE   This three-dimensional model of the pueblo and its surrounding landscape is the largest exhibit in the Warm Springs project. The model is open on all sides and is large enough to allow twenty-five to thirty visitors to stand around it. Constructed to scale, it's characterized by exacting detail and authentic textures. The cottonwoods that grow in the canyon bottom, the pinyon and juniper trees that cling to the cliff edges, the farm fields on top of the mesa, and the sandstone blocks that the houses are built from, are all represented in miniature. The presence of human figures, as well as those of dogs and turkeys, conveys multiple kinds of information. Included is information about clothing, animal domestication and, because these figures are also constructed to scale, they help visitors better understand the size of the village.

In several locations around the model are stations that pose questions that allow visitors to interact with the exhibit. They can, for example, discover the building sequence of the village by pressing a button that gradually lights up the various sections of the pueblo in the order in which they were constructed. At another of these stations, visitors can learn about architectural variation within the site. Interactive buttons highlight, for example, where all the underground structures are located, or the location of all of the towers. Visitors can also learn about differences in the kinds of artifacts located in various parts of the site. At still another station, they can put on headphones to hear pueblo elders give information about the villages, using their native languages. Other stations allow visitors to locate water sources, possible farm fields, and roads or paths leading out of the pueblo.

Situated around the model are a number of computer kiosks that allow visitors to explore questions in greater depth and wander into the world beyond the pueblo. These kiosks are linked to a large database that contains the research results from archaeological research at Warm Springs Pueblo. Visitors can query the database using sets of programmed questions, or they may pose their own questions within the parameters provided. Someone who wishes to look more closely at the building sequence for the pueblo can watch an animation of the pueblo's construction. As the cursor is moved across the time line, new structures appear on the screen. A visitor interested in learning about the archaeological evidence discovered in various locations around the village can explore this question by clicking on selected portions of the map of Warm Springs Pueblo. She or he is then presented with lists of various kinds of data; if the individual wants to dig deeper (no pun intended), she or he can click on links to digitized images of artifacts. If these artifacts are on display in the museum, the visitor might be given information for locating them. Perhaps a visitor is interested in how the Warm Springs Pueblo is related to other ancient villages from the same time period. In this case, she or he can view a map of the region that identifies the approximate locations of other contemporaneous villages and outlying small sites. A zoom feature allows the visitor to focus in on the Warm Springs community or move out to view all of the large settlements in the region.

ARTIFACT EXHIBITS Several artifacts from the excavations at Warm Springs are on display in the museum. Particularly prominent are a number of ceramic vessels of various shapes and sizes. Because these vessels are not all from the same context, they are not presented in the same display cases. A combination of murals, photographs, and three-dimensional objects used in the exhibit provide information about the artifacts original context and inferred use. For example, a small rectangular black-on-white ceramic box, the kind often referred to as a feather box, appears on a hard-packed dirt surface. Next to the box is a slightly curved portion of a sandstone wall with a niche that looks like the one in which the box was found. A couple of other small black-on-white jars with lids (kiva jars) are placed beside the rectangular box. Adjacent to the case are photographs showing the artifacts in place during the excavation and an artist's interpretation of what the room might have looked like when it was occupied. A computer kiosk allows visitors to learn about how the pottery was made, including video clips of a modern-day potter replicating the process. Other options include links to the archaeological database showing where, within the village, the artifacts were excavated and how the information gained contributes to archaeological interpretations. Visitors may also obtain information about similar vessels found in the region and learn about their contexts.

Similar exhibits featuring other types of artifacts from the Warm Springs Pueblo can also be found in the museum; included are exhibits that feature ground stone tools, cooking and storage pots, textiles (woven sandals, mats, and a portion of a turkey feather blanket), and more exotic materials (trade items, beads, game pieces, bone whistles).

Each exhibit displays artifacts against a backdrop of authentic textures and materials such as hearths, hard-packed dirt floors, sandstone walls, and mealing bins. These materials are simple and subtle in nature but they convey a dramatically different message than do the traditional sterile displays or the dark velvet cloths that call to mind notions of treasure. Computer kiosks are associated with each of the exhibits and, as with the black-on-white pottery exhibit, the kiosks address the general kinds of questions that visitors have but they also link to the artifact database and to video clips that demonstrate the processes that led to the production of the artifacts. Near each exhibit are materials and instructions that provide hands-on opportunities for experiencing some of the tasks of daily life in the thirteenth-century world of the ancestral Pueblo people, such as weaving, processing yucca, and making stone or shell beads.

THE WARM SPRINGS PUEBLO RESEARCH PROJECT   The archaeological research at Warm Springs Pueblo, which was conducted over a four-year period, was carried out by a private institution. The research findings are conveyed through a twenty-minute video shown at regular intervals throughout the day in the museum's auditorium. The video is structured by the research questions that led the excavations at Warm Springs and features the archaeologists who led the research project, as well as several Pueblo elders. The archaeologists and the elders alike provide their interpretations of life at Warm Springs Pueblo. A narrator summarizes and clarifies these interpretations, where they merge, where they diverge, and where they compliment each other. The video closes with the narrator identifying questions in need of further study; this is done in a manner meant to leave the visitor intellectually engaged rather than with the feeling that the "experts" have figured everything out.

THE WARM SPRINGS PUEBLO SITE TOUR   Visitors may tour the Warm Springs Pueblo either with a member of the museum staff or independently. A guidebook is available for visitors who wish to explore the site on their own; an audio tour that can be borrowed or purchased from the museum is also available. Most of the site is a series of rubble mounds and depressions situated around the head of the canyon. Except for one set of rooms and the underground pit structure associated with them, the village is covered by the organic matter and soil that has grown or been deposited over the last 700 years. Areas that were excavated during the research process have all been backfilled, with the exception of the one suite of rooms that has been left open and stabilized. This area was left open to give visitors an example of what archaeologists believe would have been the living space for one family. This open area also helps visitors understand the size of a typical room and helps them visualize what the numerous rubble mounds and depressions represent. People often have difficulty with the mental transformation of these piles of stone into sandstone structures. The exposed structures provide evidence that the sandstone rubble piles represent more than an active imagination.

Before the tour begins, visitors are given guidelines for visiting the site. These address issues of safety, preservation, and respect. Visitors also receive information about the ownership of Warm Springs Pueblo, its management, and the laws that protect the site.

Regardless of the form in which the tour occurs, whether with a member of the museum staff, the audio guide, or the guidebook, the structure and content of the tour are much the same. Each format has advantages and disadvantages. By posing questions during the staff-guided tour, visitors have an opportunity to gain information that is not offered in the guidebook or on the audio cassette. On the self-guided tours, visitors can move at their own pace, allowing more time for reflection and for in-depth observations. In many cases, site tours tend to be little more than an archaeological show and tell. On such tours, the guide leads visitors in a linear fashion through the site, telling them about what was found at each of the stops. I wouldn't say that this kind of tour has no educational value, but it can be difficult for visitors to assimilate and make sense of information that is not organized within a larger, more meaningful framework.

To help visitors construct meaning of the information, the Warm Springs site tours are formed around the enduring understandings and associated guiding questions. Each stop on the tour contributes to the development of these concepts. For example, the first stop on the tour is on the mesa top, at the trail head leading to the pueblo. In this location, visitors get a sense of being at "the top of the world," or at least the ancient Pueblo world. Within this 360-degree panorama, prominent landmarks in all of the Four Corners states can be seen: the La Sal and Abajo Mountains in Utah, Monument Valley in Arizona, Shiprock in New Mexico, and the La Plata and Ute Mountains in Colorado. A sense of place is emphasized at this stop on the tour and is used to help tie past and present together. Included in this discussion is information about the climate, farming, water use, and aesthetic appeal. Parallels are drawn between past and present, and visitors are asked to think about how things are different on this landscape now than they were 700 or 800 years ago.

The second stop on the tour takes visitors to the spring that the village is built around. Here, visitors are asked to reflect on how the spring seems to work as an anchor for the Pueblo and to speculate on the reasons for building the village around it, keeping in mind that this is a repeating pattern in the settlement of large Pueblo villages that were constructed in the thirteenth century. This stop by the spring continues to build a sense of place and attempts to expand visitors' perceptions beyond their own personal points of view. Visitors are asked to consider social, cultural, and religious explanations as well as the practical aspects of building around a water source. Puebloan perspectives regarding water and water sources are given in the guidebook and are also included on the audio and staff-guided versions of the tour.

From the spring, the tour proceeds to the highest point in the pueblo, providing an excellent vantage point for viewing the entire extent of the village. Several goals are addressed at this stop. The first is to have visitors "see" the ancient village by matching what is visible on the landscape with illustrations on the site map that was created by the archaeologists. A second goal is to help visitors see the view from the village, which includes the canyon bottom and the corridor to the south that is created by the canyon. The third goal is to cause visitors to think about how the village was built, including the construction sequence, sources of building materials and the amounts required, the labor investment, and the organization of labor. A number of visual aids are used to enhance this part of the tour, including illustrations that show the construction sequence, a map of the canyon and surrounding area, and the way that archaeologists believe the village might have looked in the late 1200s.

Following this big picture view of Warm Springs Pueblo, the focus changes to the family unit, thus the next stop on the tour is of the excavated and stabilized suite of rooms believed by archaeologists to represent the space used by a typical household. Photographs taken during the excavation of these rooms, and of the artifacts in situ, help visitors understand how the researchers conducted their work and arrived at their conclusions regarding how these rooms were used. These photographs and the discussion that accompanies them help visitors attach real people to this ancient ruin. It also helps establish the connection between archaeological excavation and the making of history.

The remainder of the tour expands on the concepts presented at these first stops and gives visitors an opportunity to move through the entire site. The final stop on the site tour is at a very scenic location overlooking the canyon. In this setting, visitors are led to reflect on what has been learned about the Warm Springs Pueblo and to also think about the intriguing questions that are, as of now, still unanswered. Visitors are reminded that the ancient history of the Four Corners region is preserved in sites like Warm Springs. The tour concludes with perspectives from several Pueblo people regarding their view of the pueblo as a living place rather than a ruin.

Doing Archaeology: Heritage Education at a Private Research Institution

The settings for the preceding examples of heritage education—a middle school classroom and a museum—are, to a great extent, fictional. They contain elements of real places but I know of no location where the programs I describe are actually being implemented. Although these examples are not real, I believe they are realistic. In other words, I think it would be possible to achieve the kind of programs that are depicted. In this section, however, I diverge from the fictional and use, instead, a real location. Being the director of education at the Crow Canyon Archaeological Center, I would find it difficult to talk about heritage education in a private research setting and not have it come out looking and sounding like Crow Canyon. Thus, I have chosen to use the Center and one of its programs—the week-long research program for middle school students—as my example of a multi-day, informal, history education program.

Introduction

The Crow Canyon Archaeological Center's mission and a description of the campus are given in chapter 4. To more fully illustrate the context for the educational program described in this section, it is necessary to provide some additional information. Of particular relevance are student demographics and the varied nature of the schools from which the students come. These factors are significant to educational programs conducted in any informal setting but particularly so for those of an extended duration. Crow Canyon's week-long programs include forty hours of instruction. This kind of time frame allows for a somewhat in-depth treatment of the subject matter and, thus, requires a better understanding of the learners. The more heterogeneous the population, the more difficult this becomes. Approximately 2,500 students from grades four to twelve attend Crow Canyon programs each year. Many of these students are from Colorado and the other Four Corners states, but many are also from more distant states such as Pennsylvania, Michigan, New York, and California. The Center is host to many urban and suburban students as well as students from rural and even fairly remote locations. The majority of the student population is Anglo, but there are also many Hispanic students and a smaller number of African American and Native American students. The students who visit Crow Canyon come from both public and private schools. They are from traditional as well as progressive institutions, and from schools that span the continuum between them. Some of the students have had extensive classroom preparation prior to their Crow Canyon trip and, when they return to the classroom, they will be expected to in some way demonstrate what they learned at the Center. Some students will have had no previous experience with the subject matter and will enter into their studies at a more basic level. Some of the students from the Southwest will have known the basics since they were in preschool. Some students will see their time at Crow Canyon as a learning adventure and others will see it as an unusual vacation.

Teachers who bring students to Crow Canyon are asked to provide the education staff with information before the visit regarding classroom philosophy, the learning styles of their students, special learning needs, and special physical needs. They are also given the opportunity to help shape the curriculum in that they can request particular activities that they think their students will benefit from. They can also choose to omit curriculum modules that they feel are not relevant for their students. Obtaining this kind of information in advance helps staff educators better meet the needs of the diverse learners who come to the Center.

To a large extent, engaging students in learning is not as great a challenge at Crow Canyon as it sometimes is in a regular classroom. Simply being in a novel setting can spark student interest and enthusiasm. Of course, it can also serve to distract them from the educational agenda. This is particularly true for students who have come to think of field trips as a vacation from learning rather than educational enrichment. The social aspects of field trips are especially important to students. The teachers who bring the groups set the tone for how the experience will be viewed. A goal of the Crow Canyon education staff is to ensure that learning happens regardless of student preconceptions about the purpose of the trip. The secret to accomplishing this lies in the curriculum itself, the belief being that it should cause students to become actively involved, to reflect on their activity, and, through this process, become intellectually engaged and self-motivated.

It would be wrong to assume that all of the students who come to Crow Canyon are interested in learning about archaeology or about Pueblo Indian history. This might be true for those adults and young people who come of their own accord but the majority of the Center's student population is there because of choices that their teachers have made. Nevertheless, it would not be an exaggeration to say that most of the students who participate in the Center's Middle School Research Program do become intellectually engaged with the subject matter. To find an explanation for this high degree of student involvement, one would need to look first and foremost to Crow Canyon's mission and how it is realized in the day-to-day work of the institution. Every individual who participates in the Center's archaeological research program is contributing to a growing body of knowledge regarding ancient history in the Four Corners. Their experiences in field excavation and in the lab are authentic and the work that they do counts. The Center's lab director often begins class by asking participants in the middle school program if they have ever worked on a real scientific research project and gathered data that would go into a professional report. In most cases, few hands are raised but the question reminds students that they are involved in work that has real-life use, that the work is not contrived, and that they have the responsibility of doing a good job.

Enduring Understandings and Guiding Questions

The basic understandings that provide the foundation of the Middle School Research Program follow. Typically, there would also be several additional understandings related to Crow Canyon's current archaeological research design. Because the research design evolves and changes with each project, those understandings are not included here.

1. The ancestral Pueblo people were the first permanent settlers in the Four Corners region. They began living and farming in the area as early as 1000 B.C. and completely migrated from the area by A.D. 1300.
2. Some of the cultural traditions practiced by the ancestral Pueblo peoples changed across time and others continued from generation to generation. Their descendants who live in the present-day Pueblo communities located in Arizona and New Mexico still maintain some of the ancient traditions.
3. The natural environment of the Four Corners includes multiple bio regions that were maximized by the ancestral Pueblo peoples.
4. Ancestral Pueblo people probably learned though a variety of ways, including observation, experimentation, and listening.
5. Archaeologists interpret the past through material remains, using the scientific method. They also consult members of descendant communities to learn how they perceive/explain their own past.
6. What constitutes a successful culture is somewhat ambiguous but would include continuity across time and the ability to meet basic needs.
7. Cultural differences should not be viewed as either deficiencies or advances. They should instead be viewed and appreciated as the unique behaviors, knowledge, and beliefs that a group of people, located in a particular time and place, have developed for adapting to and making sense of their world.

The enduring understandings that learners should develop during the program are reflected in a set of eight questions that guide inquiry:

1. What are the major time periods in Pueblo history? What are the types of houses, food, tools, and containers that are unique to each time period?
2. How are the lifestyles of each time period the same and how are they different?
3. How did the environment influence the lifestyles of ancestral Pueblo people? How did their lifestyles affect the environment?

4. How did the ancestral Pueblo people learn about the world around them?
5. What are the different ways to learn about the past?
6. How do archaeologists study the past?
7. What makes a culture successful? Were any of the cultures we studied successful?
8. Is it important to respect past and present cultures? If so, how can we show respect?

Program Overview

Table 8.4 shows a standard schedule for Crow Canyon's Middle School Research Program. Groups generally arrive at the Center's campus on a Sunday afternoon and depart on the following Saturday morning. This particular program is only offered from May through September because it must run concurrently with Crow Canyon's field season.

PROGRAM INTRODUCTION The first evening that students spend on the Crow Canyon Campus is devoted to program introductions of various sorts, including behavior guidelines and campus life. A key curricular goal is to get an informal read on students' prior knowledge and to stimulate their interest in archaeology and ancestral Pueblo history.

After reviewing the week's schedule and addressing any questions that students might have, the instructor for the session may ask questions designed to elicit information regarding what the students know about archaeology, what they know

Table 8.4.   Schedule of Activities for the Middle School Research Program

	AM Classes	PM Classes	Evening Programs
Sunday		Arrival	Program Introduction
Monday	Inquiry into the Past	Archaeological Site Tour	Introduction to Archaeological Research: Excavation at Cactus Ruin
Tuesday	Simulated Excavation	Lab	Free Evening
Wednesday	Excavation	Basketmaker Lifestyles	Ethical Dilemmas in Archaeology
Thursday	Pueblo Lifestyles	Excavation	Free Evening
Friday	Tour of Mesa Verde National Park	Tour of Mesa Verde National Park	Program Wrap-up
Saturday	Departure		

about the ancestral Pueblo people, and what they expect to learn during their time at the Center. The purpose of the discussion is to gain an understanding of students' preconceptions.

Following this opening discussion, the educator engages the students in an activity that is designed to stimulate curiosity about, and interest in, the ancestral Pueblo history of the region. The activity is similar to the seminar described for the middle school classroom in the first part of this chapter. The outcome of the lesson is a list of questions that students have generated regarding the ancestral Pueblo people and their ancient villages in the Mesa Verde region.

INTRODUCTORY ACTIVITY Children often have difficulty articulating (or identifying) their own questions. They are so conditioned by formal schooling and what they perceive as good school questions that they can lose touch with their own curiosity or believe that it is of no value. They may believe they don't have any valid ideas and that legitimate thought is something that comes from others—books, teachers, and unknown "authorities." The promising news is that intellectually stimulating instruction can bring their latent curiosity to the surface.

In this activity, the instructor uses a historic photograph of Cliff Palace and a brief narrative of Richard Wetherill and Charlie Mason's first encounter with this ancient village (McNitt 1974:23–24) to inspire student thought and questioning regarding the ancestral Pueblo people. Following the narrative account, students examine the photograph and write down the questions they would have had if they had been with the two men when they first saw Cliff Palace. As students share their questions with the group, the instructor writes them on a list that is used to focus learning throughout the duration of the program.

Learning to See the Past

Responsible archaeological research is driven by important questions that are investigated through a careful and appropriate research design. Archaeologists must be thorough and meticulous in their observations, committed to keeping detailed records, and skillful in designing classification systems that can help them organize and understand the data that they collect. The first full day of class at Crow Canyon places students in activities that allow them to begin experiencing these aspects of archaeology and understanding how they contribute to knowledge of the human past.

The activity titled *Inquiry into the Past* is a more advanced version of the *Windows into the Past* activity, described earlier in this chapter. The two activities work similarly with the primary difference being that the time periods represented by artifact assemblages in *Inquiry into the Past* are those identified in the Pecos classification as

Archaic, Basketmaker, Pueblo I, Pueblo II, and Pueblo III. In the *Windows into the Past* activity, Basketmaker and Pueblo I are grouped together as Early Farmers, and Pueblo II and III are grouped together as Pueblo Farmers. There are many classification systems that have been developed for describing the changing cultural patterns of the ancient peoples of the Southwest. The Pecos classification is the one chosen by Crow Canyon archaeologists and, as the students in the Middle School Research Program are participating in authentic research activities at the Center, it is important that they use the appropriate system and terminology. When either the *Windows* or *Inquiry* activities are taught at the Center, a Modern Pueblo assemblage is also included to help students understand that Pueblo cultures did not disappear when the people emigrated from the Mesa Verde region.

During the afternoon of their first day at the Center, students are taken on a tour of the site of Crow Canyon's current research project. This tour has some aspects in common with the *Warm Springs Pueblo* tour, but it's also quite different. To begin, the tour I describe for *Warm Springs* uses results from a completed archaeological research project, whereas, research for the site being studied by Crow Canon is in process. Thus, the story is incomplete. Important learning goals for this tour are to:

- Introduce students to Crow Canyon's research questions and help them understand how the plan for excavation directly relates to these questions.
- Teach students how to recognize specific kinds of structural remains and help them develop an understanding of how the site came to look the way that it does in the present—the site-formation process.
- Provide students with an opportunity to experience coming into direct contact with evidence of the past.
- Introduce students to the local geography and help them understand how the site is situated in relation to the surrounding landscape and in relation to other ancient communities.

Archaeological research methods, particularly the development of a research design, are also the focus of an evening program that is conducted during the students' first full day on campus. In this program, students are involved in a simulation, titled *The Archaeology of Cactus Ruin: A Paper Excavation* (Connolly and Matis 2003). This activity is designed to teach students how archaeologists use various sampling strategies to collect the kinds of data from an excavation that will help them answer their research questions. They are also taught the concept of conservation archaeology and are allowed to excavate only eight units from the simulated site, known as *Cactus Ruin* (this is less that 7 percent of the site). The lesson was first developed by Crow Canyon lab educator, Aleta Lawrence, in 1995 and has been successfully used with students, sixth grade through adult, who participate in Crow Canyon's educational programs. It is based on data from a small site called *Roy's Ruin* where the Center conducted limited excavations. Complete lesson plans and the full set of downloadable materials for the simulation can be found in the educators' section of Crow Canyon's website (www.crowcanyon.org).

Skill Building

Before the Crow Canyon's middle school students can participate in the actual data-gathering process, they are required to participate in experiences that help them develop the skills they will need. This includes a simulated excavation that reinforces the steps in the archaeological research process, particularly the methods for excavation. It also gives students their first opportunity to really apply what they are learning in that they are expected to generate research questions and use the data gathered in the simulated excavation to try and answer those questions. In this lesson, they also become used to taking fairly detailed notes regarding the units that they are each responsible for excavating. The final task in this activity is to have students who are working together on the same site interpret their findings for the rest of the class.

Students are usually highly motivated during this activity and are reluctant to take a break, even though the lesson lasts three and one half hours. They are well aware that they are not working on a "real" site, and they can usually articulate how they think it is different from an authentic experience—sand rather than soil, more artifacts than they expect to find on the archaeological site, and they sometimes recognize that, while they were able to dig down to the level of occupation in the simulation, they might be excavating near ground level when they participate in the actual research project.

Lesson plans for conducting simulated excavations have been widely published; some are good, some are not so good. The more closely these adhere to the practices of responsible archaeological excavation, the more valuable they become as teaching tools. For a more detailed description of the way in which simulated excavations are conducted at the Crow Canyon Archaeological Center, see *Windows into the Past: Crow Canyon Archaeological Centers' Guide for Teachers* (Davis and Connolly 2000).

Before students are ready to participate in field excavation, it is important that they gain experience in identifying the kinds of cultural materials that they are likely to encounter. For middle school students, this means a half-day session in the lab where they work with Crow Canyon archaeologists to classify materials in both simulated and actual laboratory work. In a simulated activity, students learn to identify and sort pottery, ground stone, chipped stone, and animal bone. Once they have successfully completed this simulated activity, they move on to classifying materials from Crow Canyon's current research project. This requires a great deal of instructional time on the part of the Center's lab staff but it has been a highly efficient way to process the materials that come into the lab. It seems to be a win-win situation in that the students get an opportunity to participate in authentic scientific research and Crow Canyon doesn't end up with a huge backlog of materials in the lab. Equally important is the experience that students gain in identifying cultural materials before they participate in field excavation. Again, this is a benefit for the students and for the Center in that students build knowledge that they can apply in another authentic learning situation and the Center moves closer to accomplishing its research goals.

Gathering Data

For those who believe that timidity is foreign to middle school students, I would invite them to witness a group of these youth during their first experience with field excavation. To put it in the students' own terms, they know this is real, they know it is important, and they don't want to "screw up." This is not to say that they will deliver a flawless performance but they do, generally, bring a certain level of seriousness to this work that is not always characteristic of adolescents.

When the students arrive at the site, they are each given a set of tools to work with. This consists of a bucket, trowel, whisk broom, pan, knee pads, tape measure, line level, and a clip board with a form for recording field notes. They are generally assigned to work in pairs in one-by-two-meter units that have been set up by the Center's field archaeologists. Sometimes these units are inside structures but, for middle school students, they are often in midden areas.

Even though the students have already learned some of the basics of field excavation through the simulated excavation, they are given further instructions by their supervising archaeologist (usually a ratio of one archaeologist to no more than six students). The first set of instructions deals with taking and recording elevations using a line level, tape measure, and a string tied to the secondary datum. Although the students will have done this in the simulation, it is important to review and reinforce this process. It also helps students gain a better understanding of what is meant by the term "elevations" and why these measurements are so important. When students take elevations at the archaeological site, the location of the primary datum is within view and pointed out to them to deepen their understanding of what elevations are and how they are used.

Students are also given directions on how to collect artifacts and how to separate different materials (pottery and stone, animal bone, plant remains, and charcoal) into different bags or other containers. Finally, they are given initial instructions for filling out the excavation form using the context data that is written on each bag. At this point, students are allowed to begin work. As buckets are filled with dirt, students bring them to one of the screening stations where they will be assisted by the archaeologist or educator with whom they are working. At the end of their last half day of excavation, students complete the excavation form, including a sketch map of the horizontal surface of the unit in which they have worked.

To be honest, from an archaeologist's perspective, using middle school students is not the most efficient way to accomplish excavation goals. The slow excavation pace is, in part, due to lack of maturity but also to other factors, such as their desire to not screw up and their attention to the newness of all that they are encountering. This is particularly true of the natural environment that they are forced to have an up-close and personal relationship with when they excavate on their hands and knees in a one-by-two-meter unit. Even though the involvement of middle school students in the excavation process can be slow and sometimes tedious, the benefits, seen from an educational perspective, justify the approach.

Peopling the Past

Those of us who work in archaeology education are so concerned with teaching the processes of archaeological research that we sometimes privilege the process over the historical content that the process is designed to uncover. Meaning that, we are so intent on teaching research skills that we shortchange the reason that research is conducted in the first place—to better understand the histories of past peoples. At Crow Canyon, these histories, specifically those of the ancestral Pueblo people, are addressed in a variety of ways. One way is through integrating information about families, the work of everyday life, the relationship of humans to the natural environment, and contemporary pueblos into all aspects of the curriculum. However, the most powerful way is through two important educational facilities on the Center's campus—the Pithouse and Pueblo Learning Centers. Each facility is designed to represent the approximate living space for one family during the Basketmaker III and Pueblo III time periods.

Students spend a half day at each of the learning centers, engaged in discussions and activities that provide insight into what life might have been like for the people who lived in each time period. Both learning centers are equipped with some of the furnishings one would expect to find in one of these ancient houses. Educators at the Center have carefully researched the archaeological record and consulted with individuals from a variety of Pueblos to better understand what each household might have used or possessed. Included in the Basketmaker Learning Center are items such as baskets, willow mats, gourds, hearth board and spindle stick for making fire, stone tools, atlatls, simple gray pottery, one-handed manos, metates, digging sticks, etc. The Pueblo Learning Center includes some of the same items, such as the fire-starting equipment, mats, gourds, and stone tools. Pottery is also included in the Pueblo Learning Center but is appropriate to the time period in terms of style and manufacture. Other items included are an upright loom, bows and arrows, and two-handed manos and metates that are enclosed in mealing bins. The Center's education staff has also considered what the areas around these houses might have looked like and are continually working on these areas so that they compliment the structures. A shade structure was constructed adjacent to the Basketmaker pithouse to provide an outdoor work area. Small check dams have been constructed in drainages near both structures and a garden with corn, beans, and squash is in an open meadow that belongs to neither, but is relevant to both of the learning centers. In this way, one garden can be used to demonstrate the importance of farming to people living in each of the time periods.

Some of the activities that are used to help develop the enduring understandings for this program include: fire starting, weaving, playing traditional games, doing research on uses of native plants, practicing hunting techniques with atlatls and hunting sticks, food processing, mixing adobe, plastering floors and walls, and making pottery. Due to time constraints, it isn't possible to carry out all of these activities with every group, but all students who participate in the Center's Middle School Research Program are given the opportunity to experience a wide variety of these activities.

As Dewey asserted, experience alone does not lead to learning; experience must be coupled with reflection for learning to take place. Simply involving students in these activities does not ensure that they will develop the enduring understandings identified by Crow Canyon educators. Thus, the dialog that takes place in association with these activities is critical to achieving the identified educational goals and to ensuring that the ancient peoples are not left out of the archaeological study of their past.

Putting It All Together and Assessing Understanding

The final component of Crow Canyon's middle school research program is a visit to Mesa Verde National Park. There are several reasons for including this visit in the educational program: (1) it gives students an opportunity to view the largest and most well-preserved cliff dwellings in the Four Corners region; (2) the students can view excavated houses/villages across several time periods (Basketmaker through Pueblo III); (3) the Mesa Verde Museum exhibits a large variety of artifacts that help expand students' views regarding ancient technologies and the ingenuity of the Ancestral Pueblo people; and (4) it provides an excellent opportunity to involve students in the act of interpretation. Although all of these goals are important, it is the last one that I would like to focus on.

When students are asked to describe what they see at various sites, to pose questions about the sites, to determine the time period in which the they were built, to make comparisons between sites, and to compare sites at Mesa Verde with the site at which they have been excavating, it gives Crow Canyon educators an excellent opportunity to observe what students know and believe. It works as an assessment tool—an informal one—but still a very useful way to assess student understanding. The day at Mesa Verde also allows students to recognize how much they know about archaeology and the ancient history of the Puebloan people. Their ability to speak knowledgeably about the sites sometimes comes as a surprise to the students, as if they are not sure how they learned what they know. Also, they often exhibit the ability to think critically about any discrepancies between information they gained during their week at Crow Canyon and information they encounter in the park.

This visit is an effective and painless way of discovering gaps in understanding as well as identifying lingering or newly formed misconceptions. In this capacity, it provides the educator for the group with another opportunity to impact student understanding.

Program Wrap-up

The final activity in the Middle School Archaeology Program is an evening wrap-up session. The most important thing that happens in this class is revisiting the questions that students recorded about Cliff Palace during the first evening of the program. It is generally a rewarding experience in that the process helps students recognize how much they have learned during the week. Any unanswered questions are discussed and students are asked to think about why they have not been able to answer them, or they might be asked to think of what research approach could be taken to explore the questions.

Conclusion

I have attempted to illustrate how history/archaeology programs that reflect the essential points identified in the previous chapter could be designed for three different educational settings. The examples given require significant investments in terms of both time and money. For some, the costs may seem extravagant or even impossible, given the kinds of constraints that many schools and nonprofit organizations have to contend with. I have been fortunate in that the schools and other institutions I have worked with over the last couple of decades have managed to meet the challenges of time, funding, and personal energy to achieve the kinds of rich learning experiences that I describe in this chapter. The element that they have all had in common is vision—visions of what excellent education looks like and a belief that the scarcity of resources, either time or money, are not insurmountable.

As inevitable as change may be, it is too often met with fierce resistance in many educational institutions and with many individuals within those institutions. Educational organizations, whether public schools or private institutions, need to plan for change, and they need to consider who and what they will be in the future. Without a guiding vision, they will be forced to simply comply when they are faced with externally imposed factors that impact their work, such as high-stakes testing, oppressive accountability systems, and budget cutbacks. In some cases, educators or institutions may not actually want to make the kind of investment that a truly engaging educational experience requires, so constraints like the lack of time and money become convenient excuses. Canned site tours, sterile museum displays, and authorless textbooks are all easier approaches to education than those given in the examples in this chapter but I would argue that they are anything but efficient. That which is efficient generates a high rate of output in relation to the input; in this case, the output is learning. Educational programs are not "working" if students and other participants are not learning anything from them.

For some public schools in the United States, the question of whether or not they should provide engaging history and social studies experiences is irrelevant because they are no longer teaching these subjects to any great extent, at least not at the elementary and middle school levels. Social studies and history (along with art, music, and even science) are absent from the curricula of a growing number of schools in the United States because these subjects are not included in state testing and accountability, and anything not tested is deemed not important.

This leads me to a brief discussion of a general weakness I see in the kinds of programs that I describe in this chapter, including the Crow Canyon program. There is an intuitive sense that educational programs like these have some powerful learning outcomes, and I would agree with this. However, the very practical truth is that something more substantial is needed to support this claim. Isolated studies, such as the one that I describe at length in this book, are of enormous value and provide much needed insight. However, many more studies, in a wide variety of settings, are needed to demonstrate, in a convincing way, that such experiences are more than just entertainment or educational enrichment. It seems to me that those of us who have the advantage of working in innovative educational settings have a responsibility to identify and document what is learned in these settings. I am convinced that the kinds of dialogic practice and shared authority that are illustrated in this chapter are essential to the intellectual growth and autonomy of the individual and to the development of a democratic citizenry. Unfortunately, my conviction, or the unsubstantiated conviction of any other individual educator carries little weight in the highly political worlds of education and history. Therefore, I encourage all readers who recognize aspects of their own institution or their own instruction within the pages of this chapter to build methods of sound assessment into their educational programs. The following and final chapter of this book offers some successful strategies for accomplishing this.

Note

1. "Of, pertaining to, or originating in the Americas before the voyages of Columbus." *Webster's II: New Riverside University Dictionary* (The Riverside Publishing Company, 1994), 926.

Understanding Understanding: Some Tools for Qualitative Inquiry

A major limitation of educational research has been the weak or inappropriate evaluation tools employed.

(NOVAK 1998:16)

Introduction

THROUGHOUT THIS BOOK I HAVE ATTEMPTED to both show and tell why assessment, or evaluation, or educational research, or whatever term one chooses to use, is important to programs that teach about the human past. I have discussed the always political environment in which history education is situated and ways that history can be appropriated to serve a great many different agendas. I have examined how the teaching of history can, and does, vary across formal and informal education settings. I have looked at the disconnect between the fascination that most adults seem to have with history and the negative attitudes toward history at the precollege level. But, primarily, I have focused on the construction of historical knowledge and on the importance of trying to understand how individuals, particularly children, make meaning of the past. I hope I have not depicted this as a simple matter that can be understood through one, or even a few, research projects. A body of literature is forming, but much more is needed from both formal and informal education settings. I hope that the practical nature of this last chapter will be useful to those who are interested in participating in this endeavor to understand understanding.

This chapter is, in some ways, like a sidebar in that it is relevant to the rest of the book but tangential to the central issues. Here, I provide support for investigating learner constructions of the past by identifying what I have found to be the most useful methods for gathering data and explaining how and why I have used them. These methods are concept mapping, interviewing, and observing. If you prefer, you can also think of these as assessment tools. Assessment is a common practice in education and this term may be more user friendly than "research." I am comfortable with either.

What this chapter is not, is a detailed plan for conducting a full-blown research project; none of these methods alone are sufficient for developing a comprehensive understanding of learning in any given situation. However, I think that they are integral pieces of such projects and that they can be useful individually for discovering trends and patterns, as well as for identifying key cognitive constructs. Each also serves as an effective tool for formative assessment, where the goal is to monitor programs as they are being conducted and to make modifications as needed. In a sense, they—concept mapping, interviewing, and observing—are all windows into the construction of knowledge and the making of meaning. And what we see depends to a large extent on how large the windows are and how many of them are available to us.

You will note, and it probably comes as no surprise, that all of the methods discussed here are qualitative in nature. This doesn't mean that I see no value in quantitative studies. I am simply making the assumption that anyone interested in understanding understanding realizes that this cannot be accomplished through quantitative approaches. Quantitative methods can help identify those issues that require more extensive investigation and they can help define the focus for inquiry but they are not useful for describing process or for unpacking the complex layers of meaning making.

Concept Mapping

I have referred to concept maps in previous chapters and identified how I used them to gather data in the southwest Colorado case study. In this section, I provide information regarding the design of concept maps, the various types, and their uses in qualitative research.

The development of concept mapping is credited to Joseph D. Novak and a group of researchers who, in the early 1970s were looking for a way to document what children know about a domain of knowledge before and after instruction. Concept maps show key ideas and relationships between ideas (Novak 1998). Since then, concept mapping has gained wide recognition in education, but also across many other disciplines. Concept maps are like other kinds of graphic organizers in that they make visual that which can be conceptually complex. They also have the power to illustrate the way in which the "map maker" structures his or her knowledge regarding a particular idea. For these reasons, concept maps are powerful educational tools that can be used for assessment, as a means to organize curricular content, as a way to view the process of knowledge construction, and as a learning tool.

Creating Concept Maps

The construction of concept maps is, from my experience, comparatively easy to teach. However, I should point out that my experience with doing so is primarily limited to teaching the skill to elementary-aged students. Novak points out that young children learn quickly how to make good concept maps, whereas older students often have difficulty doing so. He attributes this, in part, to their years of habit with rote learning (Novak 1998). In my southwest Colorado case study, I taught students how to construct concept maps in the context of a subject that was familiar to all of them—their town. From this group effort, students had no trouble creating their own concept maps of ancestral Pueblo life.

Since Novak first introduced concept maps, they have experienced wide use as well as some minor adjustments, usually depending on their specific use. The initial step in the construction of a concept map is the identification of a focus question that pertains to issues, problems, or knowledge domains that are to be investigated or explored. An additional number of concepts related to the main question also need to be identified (approximately ten to twenty). Because the maps are hierarchical in nature, these concepts should be ranked from the most inclusive to least inclusive. These terms should ideally be one word but no more than two or three words each. If it becomes too difficult to rank order the concepts, it may be that some thought needs to be given to the initiating idea or question. A number of ways have been devised to facilitate the ranking process, ranging from writing each concept on a Post-it note that can be easily moved around, to sophisticated software that allows the same flexibility.

The map is formed by placing the most inclusive concepts at the top of the page. This should be limited to two or three concepts. A simple map will generally have only one concept at the top; I highly recommend starting with this kind of map. Next, subtopics are selected and placed underneath the broader concepts that they are directly related to. This should be limited in number, probably no more than four or five. If a large number of subtopics are listed under each concept, this may indicate that another level of hierarchy is needed. It is likely that there will be several levels of hierarchy within one map.

The next stage of development in a concept map is to look for relationships between concepts and illustrate these relationships by connecting the concepts with lines. Linking words that further define the relationships should be written on the lines between the concepts. Together, the concepts, the links, and the linking words create meaning. Another stage of development can be the inclusion of examples under each of the concepts. As an individual views and reviews a concept map that he or she has constructed, it is likely that a new structure or variation on the structure will be recognized. This is not only acceptable it is, hopefully, unavoidable. This is an indicator that knowledge is dynamic and constantly under construction. It is their power to reflect the ever-changing nature of knowledge that makes concept maps such excellent tools for monitoring conceptual change.

Concept Maps as Assessment Tools

> In my view, concept maps are the most powerful evaluation tools available to educators, but they can be used only when they are also first used to facilitate learning.

(NOVAK 1998:192)

As with any other type of evaluation instrument, concept maps must be considered in terms of their reliability and validity. Validity is probably the easier of the two to deal with; the validity of a well-constructed concept map should be readily apparent. The evaluator should be able to easily recognize whether or not the concepts and linkages are logically sound.

The reliability of a particular evaluation instrument is generally determined by comparing its results with those from other instruments or methods whose reliability has already been established. Novak and others have compared results from concept maps with those from clinical interviews—a widely recognized method for evaluating changes in an individual's conceptual framework. These comparisons have shown that concept maps are as revealing of cognitive structures as are clinical interviews (Novak 1998:194).

When concept maps are just one of the methods used in a larger qualitative research project, their reliability can be determined in relation to the other methods that are also being used. This practice, known as triangulation, ensures that questions and issues are examined in at least three different ways. Some common strategies for achieving this are through: (1) multiple and varied forms of data collection (such as observations, clinical interviews, and document review); (2) by having multiple evaluators examine the data; (3) mixing evaluation methods (qualitative and quantitative); and (4) theory triangulation, where the data are viewed through multiple perspectives.

In the study that I conducted in southwest Colorado, I found the concept maps useful for indicating the range of prior knowledge and misconceptions that students possessed regarding the ancestral Pueblo people. After defining this range of knowledge, I was able to use the maps to sort students into categories that fell along this continuum. From these groupings, I selected fifteen students for in-depth clinical interviews (see chapter 3). Without the concept maps, I might have selected the students in a more random manner and I might not have seen a great deal of variability. To better understand how the children were constructing the past, I needed to see the full spectrum of ideas and beliefs that they possessed; their concept maps allowed me to do this.

The concept maps also served as one of the focus areas for the interview. When I showed students their concept maps and asked them to tell me about them, I gained insight into their privately held knowledge and theories. I also learned a great deal about things that I might have misinterpreted because I did not understand the imagery as the children did. To a large degree, the concept maps allowed us to have the kind of conversation about the children's thought processes that would not have been possible otherwise.

The other way that I used concept mapping as an assessment tool in the project in southwest Colorado was as an indicator of conceptual change. Students constructed concept maps at the initial stage of the project and revised them as one of the closing activities. They were given the option of constructing a new map or using colored pencils to indicate changes on the old maps. I still have questions as to whether I should have asked them all to draw new maps rather than give this option. In retrospect, I could have learned more about this question if I had given different directions to different classrooms. That is, I could have had one class make revisions; I could have had another class make new maps; and I could have given a third class the option of creating a new map or revising their old one. Although I have not used any of the software that is currently being produced for creating concept maps, I can see how useful it would be for an exercise like this.

Interviews

> Go forth and question. Ask and listen. The world is just beginning to open up for you. Each person you question can take you into a new part of the world. For the person who is willing to ask and listen, the world will always be new. The skilled questioner and active listener know how to enter into another's experience.

> (PATTON 1990:278)

An underlying assumption regarding the use of interviews in qualitative research is that the perspectives of others are both meaningful and knowable. Further, there is the assumption that these internal perceptions can be made explicit through discourse. Novak has described interviewing as a conversation with a purpose

(1998). Patton defines that purpose, saying that interviews are conducted to find out what is in and on someone else's mind (1990:278). Interviews are used as a means of data collection in a number of different academic fields such as anthropology, sociology, psychology, oral history, educational research, and journalism. Interviews have always been central to certain of these disciplines but relegated to the category of "just anecdotal" in others, thus implying that information gained in interviews is untrustworthy, subjective, and unreliable. Disciplines that have depended on interviews for their research data, such as oral history, were frequently accused of being unscientific, meaning that their work was not considered sound and was not to be taken seriously. From my perspective, such positions reflected a lack of respect for the "objects" of the research and denied the value of their perspectives. The growing acceptance of qualitative research across disciplines indicates an overall positive change in this relationship. Interviewing plays a vital role in the qualitative research process and the more widespread it has become, the more we see that it can yield valid and reliable information.

Many excellent resources are available that provide very detailed information on the construction of interviews (see Novak and Gowin 1984; Patton 1990). In this section, I discuss some of the fundamentals of interviewing and why I see them as essential to understanding how people construct historical knowledge and meaning.

Selecting Interview Participants

Because interviews are so costly in terms of both time and money (the standard ratio for transcription time to interview time is 4:1), the selection of interviewees or respondents requires very careful consideration. If I were to equate it to archaeological research, I would say that the selection of respondents would be similar to identifying where an excavation could best be located in order to answer the designated research questions. The general population included in the study would equate to the entire archaeological site, and the individuals chosen for interviews would be the specific excavation units within the site. Excavating the entire site would be unreasonably expensive and unnecessary, thus, various sampling strategies are used, including judgment and randomness. In many cases, particularly on a very large site, a completely random strategy will not yield the needed information because the units are not situated in places that include information relevant to the research questions. Judgmental samples, however, are based on some form of prior information, such as the surface remains or remote sensing data.

Relating this method to the selection of interview participants, the researcher may select a random sample but, again, this will be dependent on the size of the group. In a classroom of twenty students, a random selection of ten to twelve will likely provide a sufficient sample. However, if the group size is 100 or more, a judgmental sample would probably be more appropriate. This judgmental sample might be selected based on the researcher's observations of the group she or he might choose to use.

While selecting interview participants, it is also important to remember to include members of the program's various constituent groups. This could include the institutional perspective and the perspective of program developers and educators who deliver programs, as well as the participants themselves. Factors like the age of the participants, their culture, language, etc., should also be considered in the interview-planning process. In many cases, some kind of informed consent may also be necessary but, for minors, this must be in the form of parental consent. Teachers don't have the authority to give consent for individual interviews with the students in their classes, nor do they have the authority to conduct such interviews themselves. Many school districts have specific policy statements addressing this. Other things to consider during the planning phase are confidentiality, data access and ownership, and reciprocity—what will the interviewee gain from participation in the study?

Interview Structure and Questions

Interviews can be classified according to one of several types; these fall on a continuum from the very structured to the very unstructured. At the highly structured end would be the closed, fixed response interview. In this type of interview, all respondents are asked the same questions, which are always worded in the same way and asked in the same order. Respondents are expected to select from a set of predetermined answers. On the other end of the spectrum is the informal conversational interview. These interviews are informal and highly open ended. Questions and topics are determined in the course of the interview. Falling somewhere between these extremes are interviews that use guides of predetermined open-ended questions or topics. The questions may or may not be standardized, and the sequence in which they are asked may or may not be strictly adhered to, depending on where they fall between the formal and informal extremes of the continuum. There are strengths and weaknesses to each of these approaches (Patton 1990:288–89).

If some kind of guided or formal interview is being conducted, the type and number of questions, their wording, and their sequence will need to be determined in advance. The length of the interview also needs to be predetermined; this is true regardless of whether it is formal or informal. The types of questions that can be asked generally fall into the following categories: questions about activity or behavior, knowledge questions, questions about values or opinions, demographic questions, and sensory questions. Sometimes objects such as artifacts, paintings, or other kinds of images may be used as part of the interview. Respondents may be asked questions about the item or even asked to create something related to it. For example, in the southwest Colorado case study, I asked students to select an artifact replica about which they were to create a story.

A logical sequence can usually be determined for the different types of interview questions. As a general rule, questions of a controversial nature should not be asked in the beginning, nor should demographic questions. The reasons for not beginning with controversial or provocative questions should be obvious. Using questions about demographics at the beginning can also be counterproductive in that they are perceived as boring and encourage participants to provide only short answers. Questions set in the present are often the easiest for people to answer and are, thus, the most appropriate opening questions.

Conducting the Interview

The primary goal of any interview is to get the respondent to talk. Doing so requires that the individual, or individuals in the case of focus group interviews, feels relaxed and comfortable. The setting itself contributes to this, but much of the interview tone is set by establishing a feeling of mutual respect. Respondents must feel as if they are being interviewed, not interrogated. Rapport can be established in a number of ways. One of the most effective is to build feelings of familiarity and friendliness before the interview. For example, in the southwest Colorado case study, I spent at least two weeks getting to know the students and letting them get to know me before I began the interviews. Interestingly, in that study, the students themselves helped build a positive tone for interviews in that those who were interviewed first told other students that the interview was fun. Where a prior relationship cannot be built, time needs to be allowed at the beginning of the interview for informal conversation.

Another important aspect of establishing rapport in an interview is to keep the language used in the questions appropriate to the audience. The language should be clear but not condescending. In all cases, respondents should be given information about what to expect in the interview, details about the purpose of the interview, and who will have access to it; they should be informed regarding issues of confidentiality and they should be thanked for their contribution to the study.

Once the interview has begun, the predetermined structure should guide the process. However, I think a certain degree of flexibility is essential to skillfully conducted interviews. Fundamental to this is the art of listening. This would obviously include listening to what the interviewee is saying but I am also referring to listening for things that need clarification, that are insightful, or that may be key to unlocking some critical piece of the study. Sticking to the predetermined time frame is also important but, again, the structure should never be so rigid that it is privileged over the research goals of the interview. And, in turn, the research goals should never be prioritized over the concerns of the interviewee. To illustrate, I was once conducting a study to try and understand why volunteers donated so much of their time to North Carolina's State Office of Historic Preservation. In one of those interviews, the first question that I posed of a senior gentleman sparked an hour-long story of his history with history and his fascination with things from the past. It would have been foolish to stop him so that I could ask my questions (which his story addressed anyway) or so that I could fill the interview quota I had set for myself.

During the interview, it is important that the respondent feels that he or she is involved in a conversation rather than a monologue, meaning that the researcher needs to be attentive and responsive. Thus, interview notes should be descriptive of what is observed rather than an exact transcript of what is heard. The use of a high quality audio recorder with external microphone frees the researcher so that he or she can be fully present during the interview. The use of high-quality video recording equipment allows the researcher to concentrate even more fully on the interviewee. A time and place should be set aside just after the interview for writing down additional thoughts and observations concerning the interview.

Observations

In numerous places throughout this book, I have referred to the situated nature of learning, that is, the belief that knowledge construction occurs within a particular context. Given this, it would be difficult to imagine how learning could be studied and understood without taking a close look at the context in which it is situated. This is the primary purpose of observation—to paint a picture of the setting in which learning takes place and thereby place knowledge construction within a holistic frame.

There are many other reasons to include observation in the design of a research or assessment project. Sometimes researchers can learn about things through observations that are not talked about informally or in interviews. This is particularly true for sensitive topics. Additionally, the insiders or participants in a study will not see the same things that the researcher will see. This doesn't mean that they see less clearly or that their perspective is less valid, just that it is a partial view. The researcher's view will be partial as well, but by simply being less familiar with the various aspects of the educational program, the researcher may be able to see things that participants or insiders are not consciously aware of—things that insiders tend to take for granted. For example, the terminology or jargon used within a particular field of study is often taken for granted by professionals within that field. To illustrate, if an archaeologist who specializes in the Southwest were giving a site tour for a group of visitors, it would not be uncommon to hear her or him use terms such as pit structure, room block, natural and arbitrary strats, side-notched point, deflector, cultural fill, and dendro samples. This language is so common to archaeologists that it is taken for granted and it may be hard for them to recognize that the visitors are having difficulty with the tour because they simply don't understand the vocabulary. This kind of communication problem can be easily detected through observations.

To provide another example of how the staff in a program or institution may not be consciously aware of certain aspects of their programs, I will share an experience I had when I was conducting a study of the docent program in a state history museum. Much of my work involved observation, particularly observation of docent training and docent-led tours. On one occasion, I was observing a docent as she conducted a tour for a group of kindergarten students. When the group came to the large exhibit that was the focus of their field trip, the docent instructed them to move closer to the exhibit and out of the flow of traffic (the children were standing several feet from the exhibit and in the pathway that visitors traveled when they moved through the museum). The children moved forward but were still not as close as the docent had indicated. I found this odd; children usually need no encouragement to "crowd to the front." Finally, the docent had them move up to touch the railing that ran along the wall that was underneath the glass-fronted exhibit. When she got them to this point, she began the discussion but, for some reason, none of the children were even looking at the exhibit. I decided to try and see the situation from the children's perspective, so I knelt beside them to be at their eye level. When I did this, I discovered that I could see absolutely nothing but the wall below the exhibit. In having the children move out of the pathway, the docent was asking them to move to a point where they could not see the exhibit that was their reason for being at the museum. From her standing position beside the exhibit, the docent could not recognize the problem. From my kneeling position beside the five-year-olds, I could.

I should make clear that I do not view observation as something that comes naturally or without training. And, while I don't believe that immaculate perception can be achieved, I do think that skills of close observation can be learned. I also believe that the most effective training is accomplished through practice. Learning how to focus an observation, write thick descriptions and field notes, and distinguish relevant detail from trivia is best learned in the context of real observations.

There are a number of different ways to approach observation; according to Patton (1990), a particular approach consists of decisions made along five different dimensions. The first of these has to do with the degree to which the observer chooses to participate in, or with, the situation and people being observed. This can range from full participation to isolated observer. Either of these extremes carries its own set of challenges. To be a full participant observer in any social setting requires a great deal of introspection in terms of mind-set, as well as in the field notes and written report. The researcher must be able to tap into his or her experience with the situation and, through this, explain to others what it is like to be a part of that particular group. What makes this approach so complex is that the role of insider is not enough, the researcher must still be an observer in a way that a typical insider of the group would not. Thus, the researcher must move flexibly between these two positions at different points during the study. The ability to deal successfully with this tension between the two perspectives depends on the experience and expertise of the observer.

A second dimension of observation is the degree to which the observer's role is known by those who would be considered insiders—how aware they are that they are being watched. Is the observer's role known by some but not others, by everyone, or by no one? Within some disciplines that utilize observation in the re search process, it is now deemed unethical to take a completely covert approach. However, others believe that full disclosure interferes with the search for "truth." Thus, this is a decision that will be influenced, to a certain extent, by the researcher's disciplinary training and associated philosophical beliefs. It will also be influenced by the nature of the particular study. There are many situations, particularly in educational settings, where it would be absurd to try and assume a covert role because the presence of the researcher in the situation would be unavoidable and would require explanation.

Another aspect of observation related to disclosure is that of the study's purpose. I am certain that there are those who would disagree with me but, for most situations, I find it highly beneficial to give participants an explanation of the project and my role as an observer. There are a few circumstances where I can imagine that disclosure might thwart the goals of the observation. For example, if a study were being conducted to assess the effectiveness of cultural stewardship education in an eighth-grade classroom, it might be important to find a way to observe student behavior on a cultural heritage site without disclosing this to the students. However, in most cases, I believe there is much to be gained by including the participants in thinking about the purpose of the research project. This is particularly true when trying to understand knowledge and conceptual change, as in my study in southwestern Colorado.

By explaining my purpose to the students in that project, I believe that I gained their trust. In telling them that they were the experts who could best help me understand what kids think and know about history, it gave them a status not usually afforded to fourth-grade students. How often do adults tell them that they are the experts on anything? The time it took to explain my purpose to the students and help them understand it was well worth the effort. Numerous times throughout the study, I recognized that the students were interested in my research questions and, as a result, truly helped me think about them by volunteering information that I would not have known to ask for and by being friendly participants in the research project.

The last two aspects of observation are very much connected, so I will discuss them simultaneously. These are the observation's duration and focus. The purpose of the study dictates the focus of the observation and this, in turn, determines the observation time frame. This is a critical piece of any research design, particularly from a pragmatic sense. The duration of fieldwork has a dramatic and direct impact on the project's budget. A fixed budget that does not allow for an adequate amount of fieldwork is generally a good indication that the project needs to be redesigned and scaled back. In other words, the correct answer to, "How much time should be allowed for field observation?" is, "As long as it takes." Given this, the focus of the field observations needs to be of such a nature that its reach does not exceed the realistic grasp of the project. The focus of field observations can range from the very narrow, such as a single program element to the very broad, such as the assessment of an entire program and all of its elements.

As in all other aspects of qualitative research, it is important to remember that people conduct observations. It is essential that the person or persons (the researchers) who are central to this process should thoroughly examine their role in relation to the observation and make their position clear in the data analysis and in any reporting of the project.

Conclusion

In this closing chapter, I have highlighted some of the methods that are, in my opinion, the most useful for trying to understand how a person or a group of people develop their knowledge and beliefs about the human past. I chose to end with the practical because my primary desire in writing this book is to inspire other educators to ask similar questions, to bring the importance of these questions into conscious awareness, and to arouse the desire to search for answers.

I am optimistic about the future of the past because I see evidence that history is coming from new and many places. The human past is no longer the private property of a few scholarly disciplines, nor is it completely dominated by a single worldview. It is an unarguable fact that all human beings have a history and it seems ludicrous for any one group of people to have dominion over all of them, or even over a single human story. I believe, as others have said, that the past is a contest of stories. I also believe that it is not a contest in the traditional sense because it is not about winners and losers; it is about looking at the stories in the context of their own creation and recognizing that, as a friend and colleague of mine often says, "The past is never really past." This contest of stories is a dynamic one that will never sit still to be evaluated once and for all. It is continually being reassessed based on new information, on the integration of new perspectives and, for good or for bad, on the needs and desires of the present. How well we grapple with this contest of stories and construct our own narratives will depend, to a large extent, on our intellectual, social, and cultural preparedness. This, then, is the charge for those who work in history education, to learn how to develop and nurture the intellectual skills, as well as the social and cultural understandings, that prepare students to become responsible mediators of the human past.

Appendix I: Data List

Making History: Data List

Community Information

Newspapers
Classroom group concept maps of "Waterville Life"
Tourism literature
Observations
Informal interviews with parents, teachers, students, and other residents
Internet sites
Local radio and television

Student Thought/Work/Activities

Individual concept maps of ancestral Pueblo life
Audio-taped interviews with fifteen students
Surveys of all students after I left the field site
Artwork related to the history unit
Worksheets provided by their teachers and Crow Canyon
Observations
Informal group interviews/discussions at the close of the field experience

Information Regarding Instruction, Curricula, and School Culture

Detailed description of settings (schools, classrooms, and field sites)
Informal discussions with principal of Dixon Elementary
Informal discussions with some of the parents

Copies of instructional guides, worksheets, curriculum standards, and books
that were used to teach the unit
Narratives written by teachers describing their classrooms, students,
instructional approach
Informal interviews with teachers
Institutional mission statements, goals, and objectives
Participation in Dixon's Parent Night/Fund Raiser Spaghetti Dinner
Informal discussions with various members of Crow Canyon's staff

Other
Daily log
Field notes
Digging Deeply. Assessment report prepared for Crow Canyon
Archaeological Center, Cortez, Colorado (Kraft and Markham 1996)

Appendix 2: Interview Guide

Making History: Interview Guide

Part I

1. What are your three favorite subjects to study in school?
2. Do you like to learn about the way people lived a long time ago? Why/ why not?
3. Have you always lived in/around Waterville? Have you always gone to this school?
4. What are your favorite ways to study history (learn about the past)?
   Read books
   Go to museums
   Visit places where people used to live, like archaeological sites
   See videos
   Hear someone tell stories
   Make or do things the way they were done historically (examples: make a coil pot, grind corn with stone tools, etc.)
   Computers
5. If you could travel into the past, where would you go? (Time period and place.)
   Why there?
6. What was life like for the Anasazi (ancestral Pueblo people)?
7. What was life like for the Anasazi compared to life for people now?
   Harder or easier?
   Did they change the way they did things over time or did they always stay the same? How do you know?

8. Is it important to know about the way people lived in the past? Please explain.

9. Tell me about your concept map. (Display concept map and ask student to explain. Ask about specific content if necessary.)

Part II

Students will be shown an assortment of artifacts associated with the cultural group known as Anasazi or ancestral Pueblo. To be included: corrugated pottery sherd, stone projectile point, yucca sandal, black-on-white mug, atlatl, and mano.

Students will be asked to take a look at the artifacts and select one to tell a story about. The story should be about who made the object or who it might have belonged to. The story also might explain what happened to the object or how it became separated from the owner.

Appendix 3: Student Questionnaire

Making History: Student Questionnaire

Teacher's Name: _____

In my research, I am trying to understand how kids would most like to study history and how they think about the human past. I would appreciate your help with this. Please read the directions that appear in bold print. I do not need your name on this paper, just your teacher's name. Thank you for your help!

Place a check mark in front of your answer.

1. I am a: _____girl _____boy
2. I would rather read: _____fiction _____nonfiction _____I like both
   Are you reading a book now that you really like? What is the name of it?
3. Did you go on the field trip to Crow Canyon? _____yes _____no
4. Place a check beside each item that was part of ancestral Pueblo life (Anasazi)
   _____sheep _____corn _____teepees _____wooly mammoths
   _____kivas _____turkeys _____horses _____bow and arrow
   _____stone houses
5. What are your favorite ways to study history? Give your first, second, and third choice
   _____Read a book with facts
   _____Read a book that tells a story but has real information about the past in it (this is called historic fiction)
   _____Go to a museum
   _____Visit places where people used to lived a long time ago, like Mesa Verde
   _____See a video about how people lived in the past
   _____Hear someone tell stories of the way things used to be

_____Make or do things the way they were done a long time ago (examples: make a coil pot, grind corn with stone tools, etc.)

_____Use a computer and special software to learn about the past

_____Use artifacts to figure out how a culture might have lived

_____Play a board game or participate in a simulation that helps you learn about people in the past

_____Other (write in your own idea)

Please write a short answer for each of the following:

6. If you could travel into the past, where would you go? (Time period and place) Why there?

7. What do you like to study in school?

8. Do any of the people in your family like to study history or learn about old things?

9. What do you like to do for fun?

10. In the space below, either write or draw the name of the "coolest" artifact you saw during your Crow Canyon field trip. If you can, try and explain why you think it is so cool.

11. In the space below, write at least three words or phrases that you would use to describe archaeology.

12. Do you collect things? What do you collect?

13. Can learning be fun? Here is a chance to give some advice to your teachers, tell us what makes learning fun.

14. **For Dixon students only:** How was the trip to Yellow Jacket different than a trip to a site like Mesa Verde?

References

Adler, Mortimer. J.
    1982 *The Paideia Proposal.* MacMillan, New York.
Anyon, Roger, T. J. Ferguson, Loretta Jackson, Lillie Lane, and Philip Vicenti
    1997 Native American Oral Tradition and Archaeology: Issues of Structure, Relevance, and Respect. In *Native Americans and Archaeologists: Stepping Stones to a Common Ground,* edited by Nina Swidler, Kurt E. Dongoske, Roger Anyon, and Alan Downer, pp. 77–87. AltaMira, Walnut Creek, California.
Appleby, Joyce, Lynn Hunt, and Margaret Jacobson
    1994 *Telling the Truth about History.* First ed. W. W. Norton and Company, New York.
Barthes, Roland
    1972 *Mythologies.* Second ed. Translated by Anette Lavers. Hill and Wang, New York.
Bennett, T.
    1995 *The Birth of the Museum.* Routledge Press, New York.
Berger, P., and T. Luckman
    1967 *The Social Construction of Reality: A Treatise in the Sociology of Knowledge.* Anchor Books, New York.
Bourdieu, P.
    1977 *Outline of a Theory of Practice.* Translated by R. Nice. Cambridge University Press, Cambridge.
Bowers, C. A.
    1987 *The Promise of Theory: Education and the Politics of Cultural Change.* John Dewey Lecture; no. 19. Teachers College Press, New York.
Brown, Kenneth. A.
    1995 *Four Corners: History Land and People of the Southwest.* First ed. Harper Collins, New York.
Bruner, Jerome
    1996 *The Culture of Education.* Harvard University Press, Cambridge.

Clark, R., J. Allard, and T. Mahoney
    2004 How Much of the Sky? Women in American High School History Textbooks from the 1960s, 1980s, and 1990s. *Social Education* (January/February):57–62.
Connolly, Marjorie R.
    1996 Yellow Jacket Oral History Project. The Crow Canyon Archaeological Center, Cortez, New Mexico.
Connolly, Marjorie R., and L. Matis
    2003 *The Archaeology of Cactus Ruin* [HTML title]. Available: www.crowcanyon.org/EducationProducts/IntroPage.htm
Csikszentmihalyi, M.
    1993 Why We Need Things. In *History from Things*, edited by S. Lubar and W. D. Kingery, pp. 20–29. Smithsonian Institution Press, Washington, D.C.
Davis, M. Elaine, and M. R. Connolly (editors)
    2000 *Windows into the Past: Crow Canyon Archaeological Center's Guide for Teachers.* Kendall/Hunt, Dubuque, Iowa.
Fitzhugh, Will
    2004 *History Is Fun.* www.educationnews.org/history-is-fun.htm
Gadamer, Hans-Georg
    1981 *Reason in the Age of Science.* MIT Press, Cambridge.
Gardner, Howard
    1991 *The Unschooled Mind: How Children Think and How Schools Should Teach.* Basic Books, New York.
Harjo, J.
    1989 *Secrets from the Center of the World.* First ed. Sun Tracks: An American Indian Literary Series 17. University of Arizona Press, Tucson.
Jacobs, Sue-Ellen, J. Binford, M. E. Carroll, H. M. Tsmith, T. Mazzo, T. Naranjo, and P. Tsawa, (editors)
    2004 *My Life in San Juan Pueblo: Stories of Esther Martinez.* University of Illinois Press, Chicago.
Kraft, Richard, and Nancy Markham
    1996 Digging Deeply. Assessment report prepared for Crow Canyon Archaeological Center, Cortez, Colorado.
Lerner, Gerda
    1997 *Why History Matters.* Oxford University Press, New York.
Lightman, Alan
    1993 *Einstein's Dreams.* First ed. Warner Books, New York.
Lipe, W. D., M. D. Varien, and R. H. Wilshusen (editors)
    1999 *Colorado Prehistory: A Context for the Southern Colorado River Basin.* Colorado Council of Professional Archaeologists, Denver.
Loewen, J. W.
    1995 *Lies My Teacher Told Me.* First ed. The New Press, New York.
MacKenzie, R., and P. G. Stone
    1990 Introduction: The Concept of the Excluded Past. In *The Excluded Past: Archaeology in Education*, edited by P. G. Stone and R. MacKenzie, pp. 1–11. One World Archaeology. vol. 17. 25 vols. Routledge Press, London.

Mañosa, Cecilia
    1999 Paper presented at the annual meeting of the American Anthropological Association, Chicago.
McNitt, Frank
    1974 *Richard Wetherill: Anasazi.* University of New Mexico Press, Albuquerque.
Merriman, N.
    1991 *Beyond the Glass Case.* Leicester University Press, Leicester, United Kingdom.
Montangero, Jacques
    1996 *Understanding Changes in Time: The Development of Diachronic Thinking in 7–12-year-old Children.* First ed. Translated by Tim Pownall. Taylor and Francis, New York.
National Center for History in the Schools
    1996 *National Standards for History.* National Center for History in the Schools, Los Angeles.
National Council for the Social Studies
    1994 *Expectations of Excellence: Curriculum Structure for Social Studies.* National Council for the Social Studies, Washington, D.C.
National Paideia Center
    2002 *The Paideia Seminar: Active Thinking through Dialogue.* The National Paideia Center, Chapel Hill, North Carolina.
Nequatewa, Edmund
    1967 *Truth of a Hopi.* Northland Publishing, Flagstaff, Arizona.
Novak, Joseph D.
    1998 *Learning, Creating, and Using Knowledge: Concept Maps as Facilitative Tools in Schools and Corporations.* Lawrence Erlbaum Associates, Mahwah, New Jersey.
Novak, Joseph D., and D. B. Gowin
    1984 *Learning How to Learn.* Cambridge University Press, New York.
Ortiz, Alfonso
    1994 *The Pueblo.* Chelsea House Publishers, New York.
Patton, Michael Q.
    1990 *Qualitative Evaluation and Research Methods.* First ed. Sage, London.
Price, Margo, P. Samford, and V. Steponaitis
    2001 *Intrigue of the Past: North Carolina's First Peoples.* Research Laboratories of Archaeology, University of North Carolina, Chapel Hill.
Ramos, M., and D. Duganne
    2000 *Exploring Public Perceptions and Attitudes about Archaeology.* Society for American Archaeology, www.saa.org.
Rosenzweig, R., and D. Thelen
    1998 *The Presence of the Past: Popular Uses of History in American Life.* Columbia University Press, New York.
Ruenzel, David
    1997 Look Who's Talking. *Teacher Magazine* (May/June):26–31.
Sando, Joe S.
    1998 *Pueblo Nations: Eight Centuries of Pueblo Indian History.* Clear Light Publishers, Santa Fe, New Mexico.

Scherer, M.

2003 Do Students Care about Learning? A Conversation with Mihaly Csikszentmiha-lyi. *The Best of Educational Leadership 2002–2003.* Association for Supervision and Curriculum Development, Alexandria, Virginia.

Scheurman, Geoffrey

1998 From Behaviorist to Constructivist Teaching. *Social Education* 62(1):6–9. National Council for the Social Studies, Washington, D.C.

Schmidt, Cynthia

1989 *Colorado Grassroots.* First ed. Cloud Publishing, Phoenix.

Silko, Leslie M.

1993 From *The Towers of Hovenweep,* edited by Ian M. Thompson. Mesa Verde Museum Association, Mesa Verde National Park, Colorado.

Smith, Shelly, Jeanne Moe, Kelly Letts, and Danielle Paterson

1993 *Intrigue of the Past: A Teacher's Activity Guide for Fourth through Seventh Grades.* U.S. Department of the Interior, Bureau of Land Management, Washington, D.C.

Swentzell, Rina

1993 From *The Towers of Hovenweep,* edited by Ian M. Thompson. Mesa Verde Museum Association, Mesa Verde National Park, Colorado.

Thompson, I.

1995 *Houses on Country Roads.* First ed. Herald Press, Durango, Colorado.

Tilly, C.

1989 Interpreting Material Culture. In *The Meaning of Things,* edited by I. Hodder, pp. 183–94. Unwin Hyman, London.

Tonkin, Elizabeth

1992 *Narrating Our Pasts: The Social Construction of Oral History.* First ed. Cambridge University Press, Cambridge.

Trimble, Stephen

1990 *The Village of Blue Stone.* Simon and Schuster, New York.

Van der Veer, Rene, and Jaan Valsiner

1994 *The Vygotsky Reader.* Blackwell Publishers, Oxford, United Kingdom.

Whitman, Walt

1959 A Child Went Forth. In *Leaves of Grass,* p. 138. Viking Penguin, Inc. New York.

Wiggins, Grant, and J. McTighe

1998 *Understanding by Design.* Association for Curriculum Development, Alexandria, Virginia.

Williams-Vinson, Ella A.

Audio-taped interview for the *Southern Oral History Collection,* University of North Carolina, Chapel Hill.

Wineburg, Sam

2001 *Historical Thinking and Other Unnatural Acts: Charting the Future of Teaching the Past.* Temple University Press, Philadelphia.

Index

About the Author

M. Elaine Davis is director of education at the Crow Canyon Archaeological Center, where she develops and supervises programs and projects in archaeology education for precollege students and other members of the lay public. She is a former classroom teacher and science education specialist. Her research examines the ways learners construct their knowledge of the human past. She also publishes under the name M. Elaine Franklin.